THE
100+
SERIES™
Reproducible Activities

Mixed Skills in Math

Keeping Students Sharp With Daily Practice and Review

Grades 7-8

By
Marge Linskog

Instructional Fair
An imprint of Carson-Dellosa Publishing LLC
Greensboro, North Carolina

Instructional Fair

Author: Marge Lindskog
Cover Design: Matthew Van Zomeren
Illustrations: Rex Schneider
Cover Photos: Corel Corporation

Instructional Fair
An imprint of Carson-Dellosa Publishing LLC
PO Box 35665
Greensboro, NC 27425 USA

ISBN 978-1-56822-861-7
04-147138091

table of contents

addition: whole numbers and decimals, perimeter, money 1
subtraction: whole numbers and decimals, perimeter, money 2
addition: whole numbers and decimals, perimeter, measurement...3
subtraction: whole numbers and decimals, perimeter, time 4
addition and subtraction: mixed practice, angles, rounding numbers...5
multiplication by one number, ordering numbers, number patterns..6
multiplication by two numbers, area, averaging..7
multiplication by three numbers, rounding decimals, factors...8
multiplication with decimals, tree diagrams, place value 9
multiplication with decimals, measurement, exponents 10
multiplication with decimals, fractions, common multiples 11
multiplication with decimals, prime numbers, time 12
multiplication with decimals, number patterns, fractions..13
multiplication with decimals, area, mixed addition and subtraction 14
multiplication with decimals, factors, triangular numbers 15
division by one number, exponent problems, rounding whole numbers 16
division by two numbers, smallest common multiples, weight..17
division by two numbers, square numbers, metric measures 18
division by three numbers, area, number patterns...19
division by one decimal, largest common factor, money 20
division by two decimals, place value, perimeter...21
division by three decimals, tree diagrams, multiplication 22
decimal division by powers of ten, volume, ordering numbers 23
decimals divided by one decimal, reducing fractions, exponent problems 24
decimals divided by two decimals, averaging, number patterns...25
decimals divided by three decimals, equivalent forms, multiplication 26
mixed whole number division, changing denominators, time 27
whole number and decimal division, rounding, liquid measurement 28
division with decimals, area, mixed addition and subtraction..29
mixed practice division, factors, measurements 30
addition of two like fractions, simplifying fractions, money 31
addition of two like fractions, order of operations, metric measurement 32
addition of two unlike fractions, improper fractions, time 33
addition of two unlike fractions, mixed numbers, patterns..34
addition of two unlike fractions, area, whole number multiplication 35
addition of mixed numbers, symmetry, liquid measurement 36
addition of three like fractions, volume, whole number division 37
addition of three like fractions, perimeter, addition and subtraction 38
addition of three unlike fractions, order of operations, money...39
addition of three unlike fractions, congruency, decimal multiplication 40
addition of three unlike fractions, area, time 41
addition of mixed numbers, tree diagrams, decimal division 42
addition of mixed numbers, symmetry, weight 43
mixed addition of fractions, volume, shape patterns 44
mixed addition of fractions, order of operations, measurement 45
subtraction of like fractions, simplifying fractions, time 46
subtraction of fractions from whole numbers, simplifying, capacity 47
subtraction of fractions from whole numbers, volume, multiplication 48
subtraction of mixed numbers, exponents, money 49
subtraction of mixed numbers, area, addition...50
subtraction of unlike fractions, patterns, order of operations 51
subtraction of unlike fractions, perimeter, decimal multiplication..52
subtraction of unlike fractions, symmetry, measurement 53
subtraction of mixed numbers, order of operations, fraction addition 54
subtraction of mixed numbers, volume, whole number division 55
subtraction of mixed numbers, patterns, time 56

subtraction of mixed numbers, area, metric measurement 57
subtraction of fractions, patterns, decimal division 58
subtraction of fractions, operations, fraction addition 59
subtraction of fractions, symmetry, money 60
multiplying fractions, number sense, fraction addition and subtraction 61
multiplying fractions, Celsius temperature, averaging 62
simplify and multiply, equivalent fractions, division 63
simplify and multiply, time, rounding 64
multiplying mixed fractions, symmetry, addition and subtraction 65
multiplying mixed fractions, tree diagrams, multiplication 66
mixed practice, area, multiples 67
mixed practice, angles, fraction addition and subtraction 68
reciprocals, length, place value 69
division of fractions, largest common factor, multiplication 70
division of fractions, capacity and weight, division 71
simplify and divide, angles, addition and subtraction 72
simplify and divide, area, fraction multiplication 73
division of mixed numbers, tree diagram, addition and subtraction 74
division of mixed numbers, metric measures, multiplication 75
mixed practice, order of operations, place value 76
mixed practice, money, multiplication 77
decimals and percents, rounding, multiplication 78
fractions and percents, area, addition and subtraction of fractions 79
percent, angles, division 80
percent, largest common factor, addition and subtraction 81
percent, time, rounding 82
percent, order of operations, averaging 83
percent, length, addition and subtraction of fractions 84
percent, number patterns, division 85
percent, capacity and weight, multiplication 86
ratio, area, smallest common multiples 87
ratio, metric measures, multiplication of fractions 88
ratio, order of operations, division of fractions 89
rate, fractions as percents and decimals, subtraction of fractions 90
probability, area of parallelogram, decimal addition and subtraction 91
probability, triangle angles, fraction multiplication 92
statistics, fractions, ratio 93
statistics, circle circumference, fraction division 94
addition equations, area, multiplication 95
addition equations, decimals, fraction addition and subtraction 96
subtraction equations, averaging, ratio 97
subtraction equations, circle area, division 98
multiplication equations, area, ratio 99
multiplication equations, geometry terms, fractions 100
division equations, fractions, addition, and subtraction 101
division equations, triangle angles, fraction division 102
mixed equations, area, statistics 103
mixed equations, geometry, ratio 104
integers, decimals, mixed equations 105
integers, triangle angles, addition and subtraction 106
addition of integers, circle circumference, multiplication 107
addition of integers, shapes, fraction addition and subtraction 108
subtraction of integers, circumference, statistics 109
subtraction of integers, area of circle, mixed equations 110
multiplication of integers, angles, ratio 111
Answer Key 112

◆ Add.

| 1. | 4,628
+7,359 | 2. | 32.78
+67.03 | 3. | 689.5
+100.36 | 4. | 14,973
+11,928 | 5. | 439.06
· 6,783
7,483.4
+ 29.11 |

| 6. | 9,879
4,300
+ 1,667 | 7. | 19.04
+ 7.47 | 8. | 95,897
+55,543 | 9. | 4,576.06
+ 6,235.89 | 10. | 46.03 + 17.2 |

◆ 11. What is the perimeter of each of these shapes?

a. 6 in.

b. 9 in.

c. 3 in.   8 in.

◆ Add these amounts.

12. 1 quarter, 2 dimes, 3 nickels

13. 4 dimes, 6 nickels

14. 1 half dollar, 6 quarters, 5 dimes,
    6 nickels, 14 pennies

15. 3 dimes, 7 nickels, 4 pennies

16. 50¢, 2 dimes, 7¢, 1 nickel

17. 9¢, 5 quarters, 2 nickels, 6 dimes

18. 3 quarters, 17¢, 5 nickels

Bonus Box:
Draw a picture of .3.

Name _____

Subtract.

1. 8,403
    -3,367

2. 96.3
    -25.8

3. 5,003
    -3,999

4. 4,321
    -3,789

5. 4.6
    -2.8

6. 40.32
    -16.89

7. 2,004.76
    -1,845.83

8. 98
    - 6.4

9. 5.03
    - .19

10. 18.
    - 4.76

11. 702.4 - 273.05

12. 14 - .23

What is the perimeter of each of these shapes?

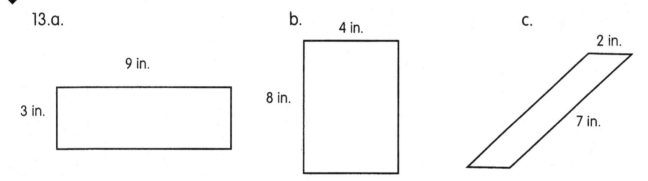

13.a.

9 in.

3 in.

b.

4 in.

8 in.

c.

2 in.

7 in.

List the coins you could use to represent the following amounts.

14. $.83

15. $.94

16. $.27

17. $.67

18. $.36

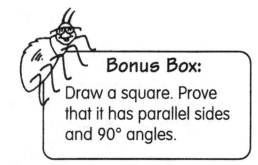

Bonus Box:
Draw a square. Prove
that it has parallel sides
and 90° angles.

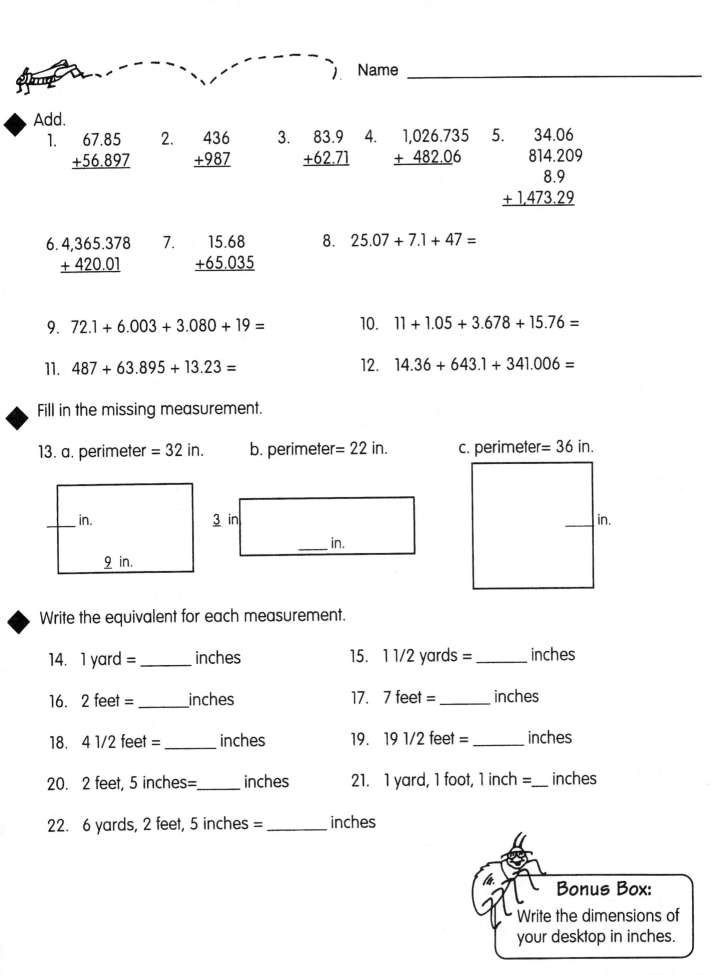

Name _____

◆ Add.

1. 67.85
    +56.897

2. 436
    +987

3. 83.9
    +62.71

4. 1,026.735
    + 482.06

5. 34.06
    814.209
    8.9
    + 1,473.29

6. 4,365.378
   + 420.01

7. 15.68
    +65.035

8. 25.07 + 7.1 + 47 =

9. 72.1 + 6.003 + 3.080 + 19 =

10. 11 + 1.05 + 3.678 + 15.76 =

11. 487 + 63.895 + 13.23 =

12. 14.36 + 643.1 + 341.006 =

◆ Fill in the missing measurement.

13. a. perimeter = 32 in.   b. perimeter= 22 in.   c. perimeter= 36 in.

____ in.

9 in.

3 in.

_____ in.

____ in.

◆ Write the equivalent for each measurement.

14. 1 yard = _____ inches

15. 1 1/2 yards = _____ inches

16. 2 feet = _____inches

17. 7 feet = _____ inches

18. 4 1/2 feet = _____ inches

19. 19 1/2 feet = _____ inches

20. 2 feet, 5 inches=_____ inches

21. 1 yard, 1 foot, 1 inch =__ inches

22. 6 yards, 2 feet, 5 inches = _____ inches

Bonus Box:
Write the dimensions of your desktop in inches.

Name _____

◆ Subtract.

1.	486.3	2.	70,550	3.	15.324	4.	19,972	5.	3.002
	-187.62		- 69,853		- 8.438		-18,995		-2.329

6. 45.5 - 32.068 =

7. 1,006 - 546.16 =

8. 98 - 17.005 =

9. 239.75 - 217.68 =

10. 19.406 - 12.947 =

11. 167.6 - 85.36 =

◆ Fill in the missing measurement.

12. a. perimeter= 35 in.   b. perimeter = 28 in.   c. perimeter = 19 in.

a.
13 in.
4 in.
____ in.
10 in.

b.
8 in.
8 in.
____ in.
7 in.

c.
____ in.
6 in
5 in.
5 in.

◆ Figure the amount of time.

13. If you start working on the computer at 10:35 AM and work for 2 hours and 15 minutes, what time will you finish? _____

14. If you go to the ball game at 4:45 PM and leave at 6:30 PM, how long were you at the ball game? _____

15. Jeff wanted to go to the 2:10 movie. If it takes him 35 minutes to get to the theater, what time should he leave home to get there when the movie starts? _____

16. Alicia rented a video that is 76 minutes long. If she starts the video at 7:30 PM, when will it end? _____

Bonus Box:
Calculate how many hours and minutes you are in school each day.

4

◆ Add or subtract.

1. 568 + 413 + 1,119 + 12

2. 618 - 615.075

3. 7.032 + 2.39

4. 10.0 - 4.003

5. 58 + 63 + 79 + 42 + 6

6. 10,000 - 3,728

7. 3.28 - 1.975

8. 54.3 + 11.43 + .78 + 6

9. 775.674 - 678.465

10. 188.273 + 452.894

11. 8.23 + 5.13 + 23.1

12. 625.43 - 620.59

◆ Are these angles acute or obtuse? Circle your answer.

13. acute or obtuse

14. acute or obtuse

15. acute or obtuse

◆ Round these numbers to the nearest thousand.

16. 45,378

17. 987

18. 4,397

19. 35,398

20. 1,059

21. 16,499

22. 9,501

23. 59,739

24. 99,999

25. 1,099

26. 145,578

27. 13,601

Bonus Box:
Draw three acute angles and two obtuse angles.

◆ Multiply.

1. 378 x 9	2. 972 x 7	3. 9,004 x 8	4. 84,602 x 5	5. 9,786 x 3

6. 700,322 x 8	7. 4,342 x 6	8. 47,859 x 7	9. 14,468 x 7	10. 4,378 x 9

◆ Arrange each group of numbers to start with the least and end with the greatest.

11. 4/3   3/4   1.3   7/6   0.67

12. 1/2   8/3   0.75   1.2   6.7

13. 5/7   9/7   3/4   0.6   0.9

14. 0.5   0.2   2/3   5/6   9/10

15. 2/8   0.74   4/6   3/9   0.4

16. 0.8   3/10   6/5   1/9   0.7

◆ Find the missing number in the pattern.

17. 3, 8, 13, 18, _____, 28

18. 2, 5, 9, 14, _____, 27

19. 5, 7, 11, 17, 25, _____

20. 3, 4, 7, 12, _____, 28

Bonus Box:
Calculate your age in
months.

◆ Multiply.

| 1. | 84
x 25 | 2. | 378
x 68 | 3. | 915
x 37 | 4. | 46,570
x 66 | 5. | 87,432
x 97 |

| 6. | 50,406
x 54 | 7. | 79,378
x 79 | 8. | 50,089
x 64 | 9. | 53,782
x 38 | 10. | 47,957
x 27 |

◆ What is the area?

11.

7 in.

5 in.

12.

9 in.

3 in.

13.

7 in.

7 in.

◆ Find the average of each set of numbers. Round the answer to the nearest whole number.

14. 6, 5, 7, 4, 8

15. 19, 17, 18, 20

16. 4, 6, 10, 5, 0

17. 43, 47, 65, 59

18. 79, 78, 80, 78

19. 94, 96, 78, 90

20. 89, 95, 96, 84, 92

21. 75, 69, 67, 77, 40

22. 82, 84, 85, 77, 70

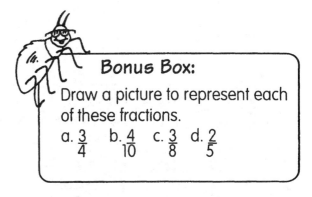

Bonus Box:
Draw a picture to represent each of these fractions.
a. $\frac{3}{4}$ b. $\frac{4}{10}$ c. $\frac{3}{8}$ d. $\frac{2}{5}$

Name _____

◆ Multiply.

1. 467 x 436	2. 954 x 896	3. 879 x 639	4. 7,683 x 604	5. 4,083 x 340

6. 60,504 x 713	7. 83,367 x 286	8. 39,976 x 764	9. 55,847 x 999	10. 40,865 x 583

◆ Round to the nearest whole number.

11. 0.863   12. 1.223   13. 6.443   14. 3.501   15. 2.681

◆ Round to the nearest tenth.

16. 11.356   17. 3.046   18. 1.483   19. 3.009   20. 5.3471

◆ Find all the factors of these numbers.

21. 20

22. 15

23. 18

24. 30

25. 21

26. 9

Bonus Box:
How many different ways can you be given coins that add to $.20?

◆ Multiply.

1. 339 x 0.46	2. 48 x 0.71	3. 607 x 0.8	4. 520 x 0.07	5. 909 x 0.15
6. 6,723 x 0.38	7. 5,507 x 0.70	8. 50,007 x 0.6	9. 9,978 x 0.76	10. 7,028 x 0.75

◆ Use a tree diagram to show the prime factorization of the numbers given.

11. 186   12. 56   13. 120

◆ Write the number that is:

14. 4 tens less than 1,183 _____

15. 1 hundred more than 17,645 _____

16. 1 hundred thousand less than 3,095,667 _____

17. forty thousand more than 65,924 _____

18. sixty thousand less than 4,397,701 _____

Bonus Box:
Calculate the minutes in your lunch period. Then calculate the number of minutes during your school year that you spend eating.

◆ Multiply.

1.	2.	3.	4.	5.
5,593 $\times 0.378$	9,900 $\times 0.74$	18,171 $\times 0.615$	32,780 $\times 0.46$	900,407 $\times 0.668$

6.	7.	8.	9.	10.
7,312 $\times 0.75$	3,251 $\times 0.23$	30,008 $\times 0.903$	7,834 $\times 0.432$	6,572 $\times 0.026$

◆ Convert the following measurements.

11. 1.5 feet = _____ inches

12. 3.5 feet = _____ inches

13. 30 inches = _____ feet

14. 60 inches = _____ feet

15. 42 inches = _____ feet

16. $4\frac{1}{4}$ feet = _____ inches

17. 55 feet = _____ yards

18. 20 feet = _____ yards

◆ Write the number represented by each exponent.

19. $5^2 = $ _____

20. $7^3 = $ _____

21. $4^3 = $ _____

22. $8^3 = $ _____

23. $3^4 = $ _____

24. $5^4 = $ _____

25. $3^3 = $ _____

26. $2^5 = $ _____

27. $6^3 = $ _____

Bonus Box:
You make a purchase that costs $6.84 and give the cashier a ten-dollar bill. List one set of bills and coins you might receive in change. Show how they total to the correct amount.

Name _____

◆ Multiply.

1.	2.	3.	4.	5.
423.09 x 0.78	92.008 x 0.607	0.937 x 45.062	0.86 x 302.07	130.602 x 0.77

6.	7.	8.	9.	10.
14.032 x 0.81	234.7 x 0.005	43. 006 x 0.4	155.04 x 0.79	5.02 x 0.684

◆ Round these fractions to the nearest whole number.

11. $\frac{6}{8}$ 12. $4\frac{1}{2}$ 13. $\frac{2}{5}$ 14. $\frac{9}{10}$ 15. $1\frac{1}{3}$

16. $5\frac{7}{16}$ 17. $3\frac{3}{7}$ 18. $1\frac{9}{16}$ 19. $5\frac{9}{20}$

◆ What is the smallest common multiple of each pair of numbers?

20. 5, 3

21. 3, 8

22. 2, 4

23. 4, 5

24. 5, 6

25. 2, 3

26. 3, 4

27. 6, 7

28. 8, 10

29. 3, 9

Bonus Box:
Write these numbers in expanded form.

365,421
59,042

◆ Multiply.

1.	0.045 x 0.43	2.	0.006 x 0.32	3.	0.978 x 0.840	4.	0.282 x 0.774	5.	0.711 x 0.84
6.	0.07 x 0.39	7.	0.432 x 0.172	8.	0.657 x 0.609	9.	0.486 x 0.724	10.	0.647 x 0.185

◆ Circle all the prime numbers in the numbers listed below.

2	3	4	5	6	7	8	9	10
11	12	13	14	15	16	17	18	19
20	21	22	23	24	25	26	27	28

◆ Complete the following story problems.

11. You meet your friends at 3:30. It takes you 15 minutes to get home and you must be home by 5:30. How much time can you spend with your friends? _____

12. Elena left to go shopping at 9:30. She got to the mall at 9:50. She shopped in 5 stores and then stopped for lunch at a mall deli at 11:25. She went back to shopping at 11:55. After making 13 purchases at the mall, she left to go home at 2:15. She arrived home at 2:35. How long was she at the mall? _____

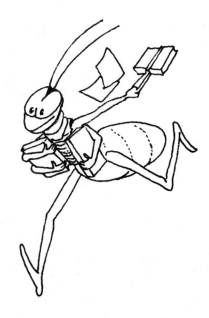

Bonus Box:

How much passing time is given you between periods at your school? How much time are you allowed in one school day to get to classes?

◆ Multiply.

1.	43.07 x 1.04	2.	100.607 x 60.03	3.	29.661 x 52.04	4.	39.098 x 9.75	5.	100.006 x 16.94

6.	2.146 x 2.65	7.	14.92 x 4.307	8.	25.68 x 4.003	9.	4.008 x 10.37	10.	45.081 x 6.18

◆ Extend the patterns by three steps.

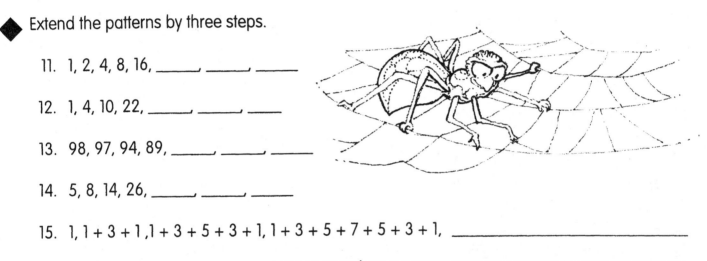

11. 1, 2, 4, 8, 16, _____, _____, _____

12. 1, 4, 10, 22, _____, _____, _____

13. 98, 97, 94, 89, _____, _____, _____

14. 5, 8, 14, 26, _____, _____, _____

15. 1, 1 + 3 + 1, 1 + 3 + 5 + 3 + 1, 1 + 3 + 5 + 7 + 5 + 3 + 1, _____

_____, _____

◆ Reduce to simplest terms.

16. $\dfrac{2}{4}$ 20. $\dfrac{4}{6}$

17. $\dfrac{6}{8}$ 21. $\dfrac{3}{21}$

18. $\dfrac{3}{9}$ 22. $\dfrac{5}{20}$

19. $\dfrac{3}{12}$ 23. $\dfrac{6}{42}$

Bonus Box:
Tell where you can find examples of squares and parallel lines in your classroom.

Name _____

◆ Multiply.

1.	46.003	2.	1.0037	3.	789.2	4.	80906	5.	.73291
	x 3.5		x 26.83		x 67.42		x 574		x 1.43

6.	463.06	7.	19.1	8.	99	9.	8005	10.	.00438
	x 4.83		x 76		x 76		x 635		x 37

◆ Find the area of these figures.

11.

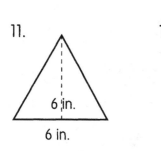

6 in.

6 in.

12.

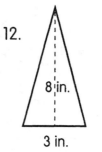

8 in.

3 in.

13.

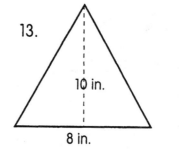

10 in.

8 in.

14.

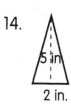

5 in

2 in.

◆ Add or subtract.

15.	4.06	16. 50,007	17.	43	18.	605.1	19. 843.9
	+3.9	- 359		-25.4		- 486.07	32.01
							188.03
							+ 4.1

20. 456 + 39 + 1002 + 87 + 42.1 =

21. 90702 - 5321 =

22. 333 + 99 + 2 =

23. 80,604 - .4526 =

24. 1,998 - 1,937 =

Bonus Box:

Using the numerical expression of today's date (example: 09/01/99), write the largest number you can.

Name _____

◆ Multiply.

| 1. | 573 <br> x 465 | 2. | 45,702 <br> x 7 | 3. | .0003
 x.05 | 4. | 78 <br> x 39 | 5. | 65.27 <br> x 33.28 |

| 6. | 3.897
 x.52 | 7. | 9,182 <br> x .004 | 8. | 7,364 <br> x 82 | 9. | 65 <br> x 537 | 10. | 3.815 <br> x 29.16 |

◆ Find the greatest common factor for each pair of numbers.

11. 28, 36

12. 12, 16

13. 9, 15

14. 12, 22

15. 10, 15

16. 10, 20

17. 6, 8

18. 6, 10

19. 3, 9

20. 7, 9

21. 4, 8

22. 5, 7

◆ Below are shown the first four triangular numbers. What is the eighth triangular number? Draw it.

Bonus Box:
Calculate the number of hours until your next birthday.

IF87124 Mixed Skills in Math

◆ Divide.

1. $8\overline{)468}$ 2. $5\overline{)95}$ 3. $7\overline{)423}$ 4. $9\overline{)2,200}$ 5. $6\overline{)4,281}$

6. $9\overline{)4,064}$ 7. $7\overline{)9,586}$ 8. $5\overline{)43,872}$ 9. $9\overline{)50,667}$ 10. $8\overline{)33,406}$

◆ Add or subtract.

11. $2^2 + 2^2 =$ 12. $3^3 - 2^2 =$

13. $5^2 + 2^3 =$ 14. $6^2 + 4^3 =$

15. $4^2 - 2^3 =$ 16. $9^3 + 6^2 =$

17. $7^2 - 3^3 =$ 18. $8^2 - 3^3 =$

19. $5^3 - 5^2 =$

◆ Use this number to answer the following questions: 235,874,927.

Round this number to the:

20. Hundreds place _____   21. Millions place _____

22. Thousands place _____   23. Ten thousands place _____

24. Hundred thousands place _____

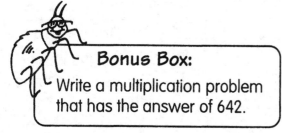

Bonus Box:
Write a multiplication problem
that has the answer of 642.

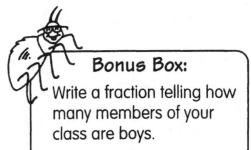

◆ Divide.

1. $23\overline{)85}$ 2. $15\overline{)54}$ 3. $62\overline{)739}$ 4. $19\overline{)2,056}$ 5. $42\overline{)867}$

6. $29\overline{)850}$ 7. $75\overline{)7,052}$ 8. $82\overline{)7,463}$ 9. $62\overline{)892}$ 10. $12\overline{)1,067}$

◆ Find the lowest common multiple for each group of numbers.

11. 6, 4, 3   12. 5, 3, 2

13. 2, 3, 4   14. 3, 4, 5

15. 2, 3, 5   16. 7, 2, 3

17. 8, 4, 12   18. 3, 9, 6

19. 4, 6, 5

◆ Write the equivalent measurement.

20. 1 lb. 4 oz. = _____ oz

21. 2 lbs. 3 oz. = _____ oz.

22. 64 oz. = _____ lbs.

23. 40 oz. = _____ lbs.

24. 1,140 oz. = _____ lbs.

25. 110 lbs. = _____ oz.

Bonus Box:
Write a fraction telling how many members of your class are boys.

Name _____

◆ Divide.

1. $46\overline{)7,892}$ 2. $91\overline{)3,005}$ 3. $75\overline{)1,003}$ 4. $12\overline{)3,602}$ 5. $17\overline{)3,506}$

6. $49\overline{)10,032}$ 7. $31\overline{)30,076}$ 8. $14\overline{)1,206}$ 9. $43\overline{)2,618}$ 10. $72\overline{)8,598}$

◆ Here are three square numbers. Please draw a picture to represent 5 squared or 5^2. Name three square numbers greater than 95.

◆ Complete the following metric conversions.

11. 3 m =_____cm

12. $1\frac{1}{2}$ m =_____cm

13. 80 mm= _____cm

14. 6 cm = _____ mm

15. 63.5 cm = _____ mm

16. 2.5 m = _____ cm

17. 34.5 m=_____mm

18. 500 mm = _____m

19. 50 mm = _____ cm

20. 2.5 m = _____ mm

Bonus Box: Write your height in centimeters.

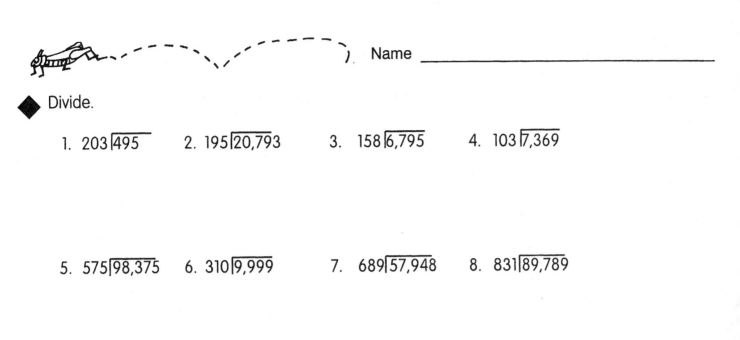

Name _____

◆ Divide.

1. 203|495̄

2. 195|20,793̄

3. 158|6,795̄

4. 103|7,369̄

5. 575|98,375̄

6. 310|9,999̄

7. 689|57,948̄

8. 831|89,789̄

◆ Find the area of each figure.

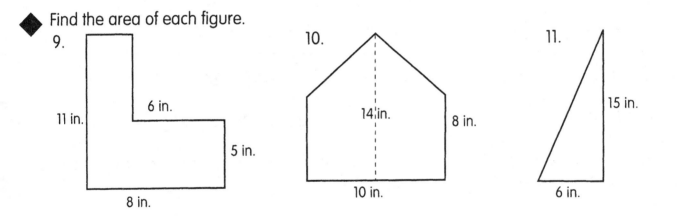

9.

11 in.
6 in.
5 in.
8 in.

10.

14 in.
8 in.
10 in.

11.

15 in.
6 in.

◆ Find the pattern and fill in the missing number.

12. 2, 5, 14, 41, _____

13. 1, 4, 10, 22, 46, _____

14. 98, 93, 88, 83, _____

15. 1, 5, 13, 29, _____

Bonus Box:
Write the area of your locker door.

Name _____

◆ Divide. If you need to extend your problem, go only one decimal place.

1. $.5\overline{)438}$ 2. $.6\overline{)782}$ 3. $.3\overline{)849}$ 4. $.7\overline{)472}$ 5. $.8\overline{)573}$

6. $.3\overline{)7,843}$ 7. $.4\overline{)5,251}$ 8. $.7\overline{)9,056}$ 9. $.6\overline{)9,007}$ 10. $.9\overline{)8,076}$

◆ Find the largest common factor of each group of numbers.

11. 8, 18   12. 27, 9
13. 63, 36   14. 49, 42
15. 27, 18, 36   16. 45, 35, 50
17. 7, 5, 9   18. 16, 12, 24
19. 18, 6, 24   20. 50, 20, 30

◆ For each of the following purchases, give the amount of change due and what coins and bills you would give the customer as the correct change.

21. Customer gives you $10 for a purchase of $6.78.

22. Customer gives you $20 for a purchase of $12.13.

23. Customer gives you $10 for a purchase of $2.85.

Bonus Box:

Print the first names of yourself and four friends. Find the average number of letters in your names. Do any of you have the average number of letters in your name?

Name _____

◆ Divide. If it is necessary to extend your problem, go only one decimal place.

1. .23⟌624   2. .62⟌45   3. .11⟌832   4. .09⟌7914   5. .81⟌570

6. .63⟌15   7. .21⟌93   8. .99⟌104   9. .15⟌703   10. .45⟌403

◆ Use this number to answer the following questions. 123,456,789.987654

What number is in the:
11. tenths place? _____

12. hundreds place_____

13. thousandths place? _____

14. hundred thousands place? _____

15. ten thousandths place? _____

16. millionths place? _____

Bonus Box:
Give the perimeter of your foot. Explain how you arrived at that measurement.

◆ Find the perimeter of the these figures.

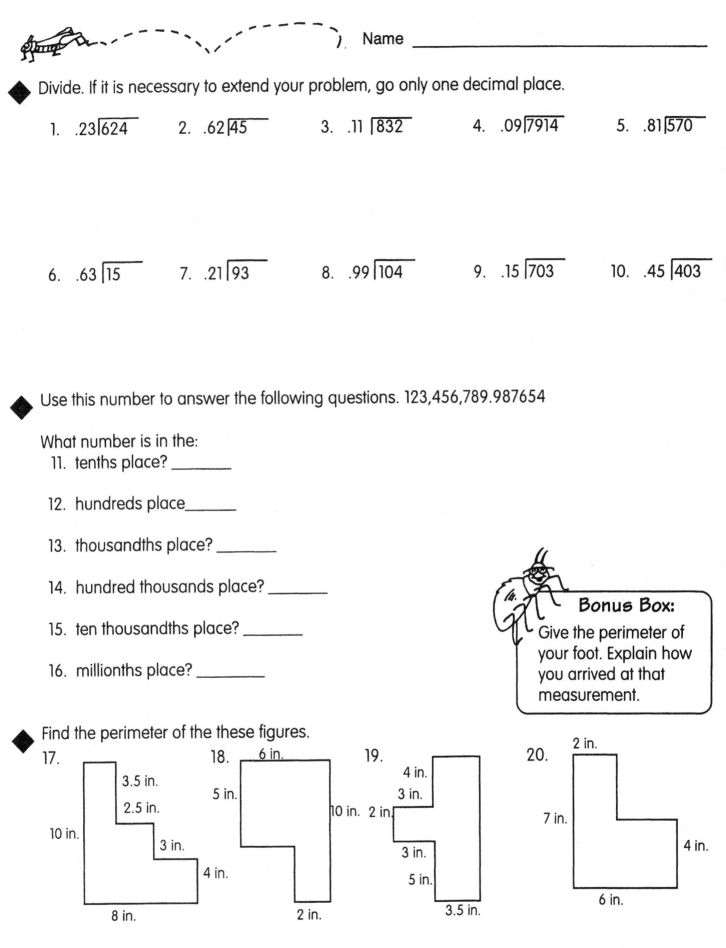

17.
3.5 in.
2.5 in.
10 in.
3 in.
4 in.
8 in.

18. 6 in.
5 in.
2 in.

19.
4 in.
3 in.
10 in. 2 in.
3 in.
5 in.
3.5 in.

20. 2 in.
7 in.
4 in.
6 in.

Name _____

◆ Divide. If you must extend your problem, add only one decimal place.

1. $.321\overline{)73}$ 2. $.076\overline{)3,627}$ 3. $.211\overline{)43}$ 4. $.135\overline{)728}$ 5. $.016\overline{)46}$

6. $.003\overline{)2}$ 7. $.999\overline{)17}$ 8. $.708\overline{)85}$ 9. $.500\overline{)82}$ 10. $.742\overline{)736}$

◆ Use a tree diagram to show the prime factors of each number.

11. 68   12. 112   13. 235

◆ Multiply.
14. 376   15. 843   16. 9,037   17. 9,018
    x 43   x 735   x 832   x 783

18. 389   19. 526   20. 999   21. 678
    x 45   x 248   x 876   x 77

Bonus Box:
Write a division problem that has 95 as the answer.

◆ Divide.

1. $467.43 \div 10 =$

2. $5.28 \div 100 =$

3. $52.4 \div 10 =$

4. $3.008 \div 100 =$

5. $213.85 \div 10 =$

6. $100\overline{)522.37} =$

7. $10\overline{)0.6} =$

8. $100\overline{)42.7} =$

9. $100\overline{)65.3} =$

10. $3{,}829.7 \div 1{,}000 =$

11. $228.1 \div 100 =$

12. $16.8 \div 1{,}000 =$

◆ Find the volume of each figure.

13. _____ 14. _____ 15. _____ 16. _____ cu. in.

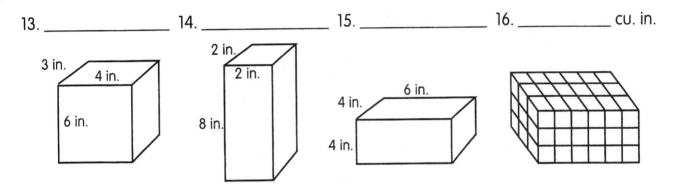

◆ Put these numbers in order from the least to the greatest.

17. 13.42, 67.4, $12\frac{1}{2}$, $2\frac{1}{3}$, 14.2 _____

18. $6\frac{7}{14}$, 7.25, 6.49, $6\frac{3}{4}$, $7\frac{1}{10}$ _____

19. 5.3, $5\frac{1}{4}$, 5.2, $5\frac{6}{8}$, 5.8 _____

20. 2.7, 2.8, $2\frac{3}{4}$, $2\frac{1}{4}$, 2.1 _____

Bonus Box:
How many different ways can you be given coins that add up to 25¢?

Name _____

Divide. If you need to extend your problem, go only one more decimal place.

1. $.31\overline{).62}$ 2. $.8\overline{)3.67}$ 3. $.7\overline{).53}$ 4 $.6\overline{).043}$ 5 $.3\overline{)1.23}$

6. $.1\overline{)75}$ 7. $.8\overline{)54}$ 8. $.5\overline{)5.93}$ 9. $.4\overline{)5.23}$ 10. $.9\overline{)3.26}$

Write these fractions in their simplest terms.

11. $\frac{6}{8}$ 15. $\frac{21}{28}$

12. $\frac{10}{12}$ 16. $\frac{15}{25}$

13. $\frac{14}{18}$ 17. $\frac{42}{49}$

14. $\frac{12}{18}$ 18. $\frac{25}{30}$

Solve these problems.

19. $3^3 \times 2^2 =$ 20. $5^2 \times 2 =$ 21. $6^3 - 4^2 =$

22. $9^2 - 8^2 =$ 23. $5^3 \div 3 =$ 24. $6^2 \div 9 =$

25. $10^2 \div 5 =$ 26. $65 - 7^2 =$

Bonus Box:

Write what time it would be in New York City if you called a store there at the beginning of this class period.

Name _____

◆ Divide. If you need to extend your problem, add only one decimal place.

1. $.34\overline{)1.06}$ 2. $.10\overline{)34.1}$ 3. $.98\overline{)1.762}$ 4. $.56\overline{)1.276}$ 5. $.32\overline{)6.7}$

6. $.07\overline{)1.63}$ 7. $.72\overline{)6.91}$ 8. $.58\overline{)3.07}$ 9. $.78\overline{)54.3}$ 10. $.08\overline{)62.5}$

◆ Find the average for these groups of numbers.

11. 43, 45, 44, 47, 45

12. 79, 78, 79, 69, 77, 85

13. 95, 96, 97, 99, 96, 85

14. 85, 83, 87, 75, 70, 76

15. 76, 77, 78, 77, 79, 60

16. 12, 14, 12, 13, 10, 11,

◆ Continue each number pattern three steps.

17. 4, 9, 16, 25, 36, _____, _____, _____

18. 150, 145, 135, 120, 100, _____, _____, _____

19. 1, 4, 13, 40, 121, _____, _____, _____

20. 1, 1, 2, 3, 5, 8, 13, 21. , _____, _____, _____

Bonus Box:
Make a number pattern for a classmate to solve.

◆ Divide. If you need to extend the problem, add only one decimal place.

1. .301 ⟌ 4.603   2. .005 ⟌ .0075   3. .090 ⟌ 4.63   4. .505 ⟌ 5.01   5. .801 ⟌ .2345

6. .698 ⟌ .973   7. .097 ⟌ 6.7   8. .080 ⟌ 2.8   9. .075 ⟌ 4.5   10. .428 ⟌ .824

◆ Give the correct fraction for each decimal and decimal for each fraction.

11. $\frac{4}{10}$

12. $\frac{9}{100}$

13. 0.75

14. $\frac{1}{4}$

15. 0.6

16. $\frac{7}{14}$

17. .20

18. .09

19. $\frac{6}{8}$

20. 0.2

21. $\frac{6}{20}$

22. 0.83

◆ Complete these problems.

23. 4.7   24. 68   25. 7.28   26.   .072
    x 6.1   x 2.9   x 36   x 3.02

27. 8.06   28. .380   29. 25.8   30. 1 68
    x 1.2   x .65   x .73   x 8.54

Bonus Box: Calculate your worth if each inch of your height is worth $15.

Name _____

◆ Divide.

1. $72\overline{)436}$ 2. $9\overline{)428}$ 3. $301\overline{)654}$ 4. $9\overline{)789}$ 5. $73\overline{)578}$

6. $652\overline{)6834}$ 7. $58\overline{)157}$ 8. $7\overline{)999}$ 9. $43\overline{)675}$ 10. $48\overline{)192}$

◆ Change these to fractions with the same denominator. Use the smallest denominator possible.

11. $\frac{1}{3}, \frac{1}{4}$ 12. $\frac{1}{3}, \frac{3}{6}$ 13. $\frac{3}{5}, \frac{4}{15}$ 14. $\frac{2}{3}, \frac{1}{9}$

15. $\frac{5}{7}, \frac{1}{3}$ 16. $\frac{2}{9}, \frac{2}{3}$ 17. $\frac{1}{5}, \frac{1}{6}$ 18. $\frac{2}{7}, \frac{2}{5}$

19. $\frac{1}{6}, \frac{2}{9}$

◆ Work the following story problems.

20. Jorge and Jerry went to play racquetball. Their court reservation was for 55 minutes. What time must they start play to be done by 4:15? _____

21. Ellen and Samantha have volleyball practice after school for 1 hour and 40 minutes. How much practice time do they put in each week? _____

22. Jeff and Sharon are working on a project together. They each worked for 1½ hours separately and then worked for 45 minutes together. What is the amount of time that each of them worked on the project? _____

Bonus Box:
Give the location of two squares in your classroom.

Name _____

◆ Divide. If you need to extend a problem, go only one decimal place.

1. $.68\overline{)43}$ 2. $.8\overline{)902}$ 3. $15\overline{)88.4}$ 4. $25\overline{)3.05}$ 5. $.08\overline{)756}$

6. $4.01\overline{)1,687}$ 7. $.9\overline{)678}$ 8. $2.8\overline{)379}$ 9. $4.3\overline{)767}$ 10. $5.07\overline{)786}$

◆ Use this number to answer the following questions. 123,456.98765

What number would you have if you rounded it to the:

11. hundreds place? _____

12. thousandths place? _____

13. ten thousands place? _____

14. hundred thousandths place? _____

◆ Write the equivalents of the measurements.

15. 2 gallons = _____ quarts

16. 12 quarts = _____ gallons

17. 8 pints = _____ quarts

18. 17 pints = _____ quarts

19. 6 quarts + 2 pints + 4 cups = _____ gallons

20. 8 cups + 8 pints + 8 quarts = _____ gallons

Bonus Box:

If everyone in the class you are in now drinks 1 pint of juice, how many gallons would that be? Do your calculations and give your answer.

Name _____

◆ Divide. If you need to extend the problem, go only one decimal place.

1. $.9\overline{)1.08}$ 2. $.06\overline{)1.427}$ 3. $2.1\overline{).685}$ 4. $.50\overline{)32.05}$ 5. $.64\overline{)6.92}$

6. $7.5\overline{)1.563}$ 7. $.89\overline{).5869}$ 8. $.003\overline{).5784}$ 9. $.7\overline{)43.4}$ 10. $.8\overline{)65.6}$

◆ Find the area of each figure.

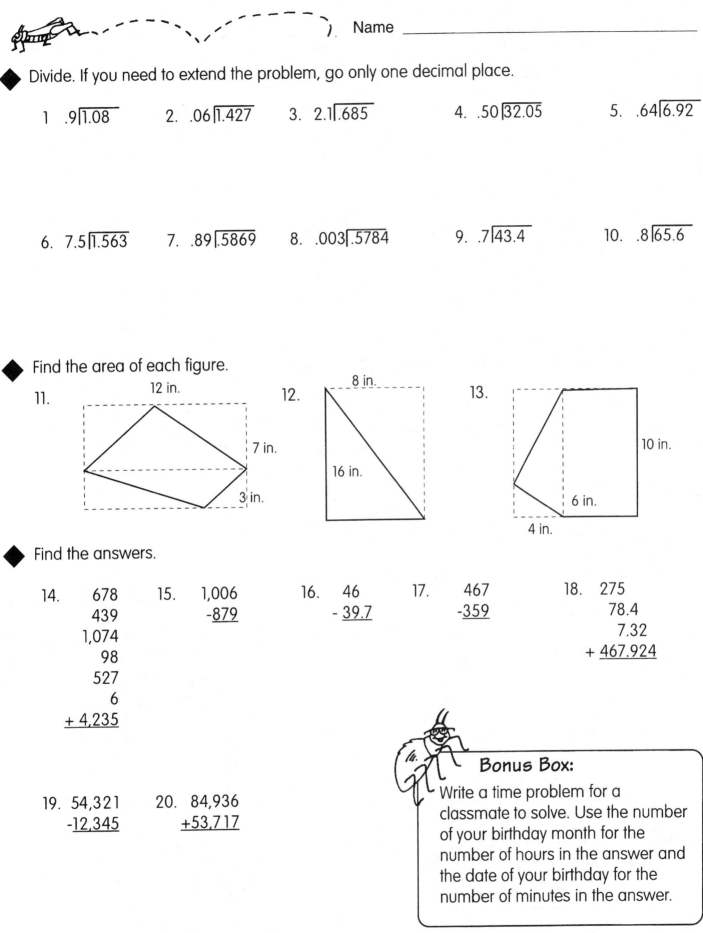

11.
12 in.
7 in.
3 in.

12.
8 in.
16 in.

13.
10 in.
6 in.
4 in.

◆ Find the answers.

14.   678
         439
       1,074
          98
         527
           6
     + 4,235

15.   1,006
       - 879

16.   46
      - 39.7

17.   467
      -359

18.   275
        78.4
        7.32
     + 467.924

19. 54,321
     -12,345

20. 84,936
     +53,717

Bonus Box:
Write a time problem for a classmate to solve. Use the number of your birthday month for the number of hours in the answer and the date of your birthday for the number of minutes in the answer.

◆ Divide. If you need to extend the problem, go only one more decimal place.

1. 4⟌64.39 2. 63⟌544.2 3. .07⟌92.81 4. 783⟌961 5. .8⟌75

6. 1.86⟌8.54 7. 7.4⟌63.29 8. 99⟌574.3 9. .08⟌168.2 10. .5⟌9

◆ Write a number that has both of these numbers as factors.

11. 5, 6   12. 7, 2   13. 3, 8   14. 5, 8
15. 2, 3   16. 8, 9   17. 4, 6   18. 3, 9
19. 3, 5   20. 5, 2   21. 7, 3   22. 6, 9

◆ Write the answer.

23. 5 feet 4 inches = _____ inches

24. 4 pounds = _____ ounces

25. 2 ½ gallons = _____ quarts

26. 80 ounces = _____ pounds

27. 90 minutes = _____ hours

28. 32 pints = _____ gallons

Bonus Box:
Calculate the number
of hours since your
last birthday.

◆ Add. Always simplify if possible.

1. $\frac{1}{4}$ 2. $\frac{1}{3}$ 3. $\frac{3}{8}$ 4. $\frac{1}{5}$ 5. $\frac{2}{9}$

$+ \frac{1}{4}$ $+ \frac{1}{3}$ $+ \frac{3}{8}$ $+ \frac{3}{5}$ $+ \frac{4}{9}$

6. $\frac{2}{7}$ 7. $\frac{7}{11}$ 8. $\frac{5}{9}$ 9. $\frac{4}{8}$ 10. $\frac{2}{10}$

$+ \frac{3}{7}$ $+ \frac{3}{11}$ $+ \frac{2}{9}$ $+ \frac{3}{8}$ $+ \frac{6}{10}$

◆ Simplify these fractions.

11. $\frac{4}{8}$ 12. $\frac{4}{12}$ 13. $\frac{5}{15}$ 14. $\frac{3}{18}$ 15. $\frac{9}{12}$

16. $\frac{6}{8}$ 17. $\frac{20}{25}$ 18. $\frac{6}{21}$ 19. $\frac{4}{20}$ 20. $\frac{4}{18}$

21. $\frac{2}{16}$ 22. $\frac{11}{22}$ 23. $\frac{9}{21}$ 24. $\frac{25}{100}$ 25. $\frac{16}{18}$

◆ Give the correct change and possible bills and coins to make the change.

26. $14.56 purchase paid for with $20.

27. $8.29 purchase paid for with $10.

28. $5.59 purchase paid for with $6.

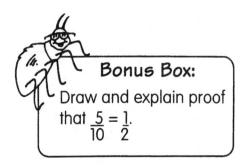

Bonus Box:
Draw and explain proof that $\frac{5}{10} = \frac{1}{2}$.

Name _____

◆ Add. Always simplify if possible.

1. $\dfrac{4}{8}$ 2. $\dfrac{5}{8}$ 3. $\dfrac{4}{9}$ 4. $\dfrac{2}{3}$ 5. $\dfrac{4}{15}$

  $+\dfrac{2}{8}$ $+\dfrac{5}{8}$ $+\dfrac{2}{9}$ $+\dfrac{2}{3}$ $+\dfrac{6}{15}$

6. $\dfrac{8}{11}$ 7. $\dfrac{3}{20}$ 8. $\dfrac{5}{7}$ 9. $\dfrac{6}{12}$ 10. $\dfrac{4}{18}$

  $+\dfrac{5}{11}$ $+\dfrac{7}{20}$ $+\dfrac{4}{7}$ $+\dfrac{9}{12}$ $+\dfrac{16}{18}$

◆ Work the following problems. Remember the order of operations.

11. $(4 \times 8) \div 2 + 6 =$ 12. $16 - 4 + (13 + 7) =$

13. $4 + (9 \div 3) + 3 =$ 14. $(100 \div 4) \times 3 =$

15. $9 + 3 - 6 \times 2 \div 4 =$ 16. $17 + 7 \times 2 - 11 =$

◆ Find the answer.

17. 170 mm = _____ cm   18. ½ m = _____ cm

19. 75 mm = _____ cm   20. 125 cm. = _____ m

21. 168 cm. = _____ mm   22. 1,000 cm. = _____ m

Bonus Box:
Write the
measurements of
your desk in cm.

Name _____

◆ Add. Always simplify when possible.

1. $\dfrac{1}{3}$
   $+ \dfrac{1}{4}$

2. $\dfrac{1}{8}$
   $+ \dfrac{1}{4}$

3. $\dfrac{2}{3}$
   $+ \dfrac{1}{5}$

4. $\dfrac{1}{5}$
   $+ \dfrac{1}{6}$

5. $\dfrac{1}{2}$
   $+ \dfrac{2}{10}$

6. $\dfrac{2}{8}$
   $+ \dfrac{2}{5}$

7. $\dfrac{2}{6}$
   $+ \dfrac{1}{9}$

8. $\dfrac{1}{4}$
   $+ \dfrac{1}{8}$

9. $\dfrac{1}{9}$
   $+ \dfrac{1}{3}$

10. $\dfrac{2}{7}$
    $+ \dfrac{1}{4}$

◆ Simplify.

11. $\dfrac{11}{5}$

12. $\dfrac{18}{5}$

13. $\dfrac{19}{3}$

14. $\dfrac{6}{5}$

15. $\dfrac{5}{4}$

16. $\dfrac{6}{4}$

17. $\dfrac{3}{2}$

18. $\dfrac{45}{20}$

19. $\dfrac{9}{3}$

20. $\dfrac{8}{6}$

21. $\dfrac{9}{7}$

22. $\dfrac{14}{3}$

23. $\dfrac{20}{8}$

24. $\dfrac{17}{4}$

25. $\dfrac{15}{3}$

◆ Work each story problem.

26. Andres and Anna can walk 1 mile in 20 minutes. How long will it take them to walk 4.5 miles? _____

27. Jerry and Gene played 9 holes of golf in 2 hours and 45 minutes. How long will it take them to play 18 holes? _____

28. Elsa and Liz thought they could fix dinner in 45 minutes. When they were halfway done, .4 of an hour had passed. Did they fix dinner in 45 minutes? _____

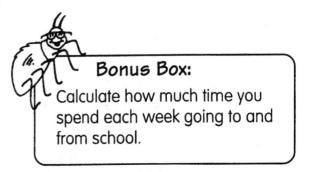

Bonus Box:
Calculate how much time you spend each week going to and from school.

◆ Add. Always simplify when possible.

1. $\dfrac{3}{7}$ $+ \dfrac{2}{5}$

2. $\dfrac{4}{9}$ $+ \dfrac{2}{7}$

3. $\dfrac{3}{9}$ $+ \dfrac{1}{8}$

4. $\dfrac{3}{10}$ $+ \dfrac{2}{5}$

5. $\dfrac{1}{12}$ $+ \dfrac{2}{3}$

6. $\dfrac{4}{9}$ $+ \dfrac{1}{6}$

7. $\dfrac{3}{14}$ $+ \dfrac{1}{7}$

8. $\dfrac{3}{5}$ $+ \dfrac{4}{15}$

9. $\dfrac{1}{2}$ $+ \dfrac{2}{5}$

10. $\dfrac{1}{3}$ $+ \dfrac{1}{18}$

◆ Simplify.

11. $4\dfrac{6}{3}$

12. $2\dfrac{6}{4}$

13. $1\dfrac{15}{4}$

14. $2\dfrac{18}{4}$

15. $5\dfrac{4}{3}$

16. $3\dfrac{8}{3}$

17. $5\dfrac{7}{2}$

18. $2\dfrac{9}{8}$

19. $1\dfrac{18}{8}$

20. $3\dfrac{9}{2}$

21. $2\dfrac{27}{3}$

22. $3\dfrac{15}{4}$

23. $4\dfrac{29}{7}$

24. $3\dfrac{19}{5}$

25. $13\dfrac{12}{9}$

◆ Complete each pattern.

26. 1, 3, 6, 10, 15, 21, _____, _____

27. 1, 2, 4, 8, 16, 32, _____, _____

28. 1, 3, 9, 27, 81, _____, _____

29. 7, 14, 21, 28, 35, _____, _____

30. 1, 3, 7, 13, 21, _____, _____

31. 1, 5, 25, 125, 625, _____, _____

Bonus Box:
Find the average of the ages of all the members of your family.

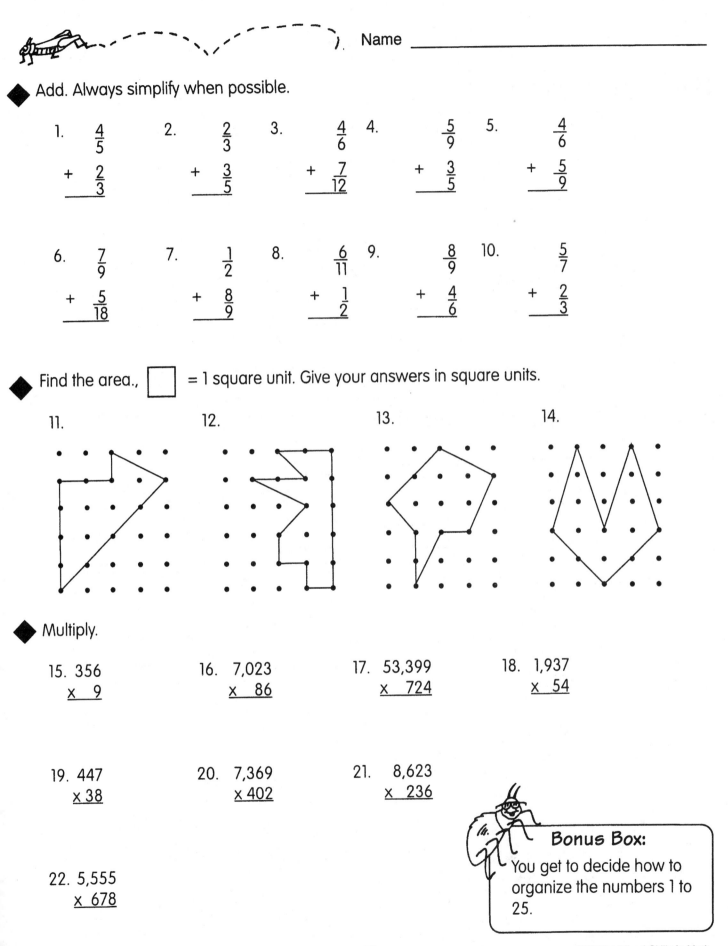

Name _____

◆ Add. Always simplify when possible.

1. $\frac{4}{5}$
   $+ \frac{2}{3}$
   _____

2. $\frac{2}{3}$
   $+ \frac{3}{5}$
   _____

3. $\frac{4}{6}$
   $+ \frac{7}{12}$
   _____

4. $\frac{5}{9}$
   $+ \frac{3}{5}$
   _____

5. $\frac{4}{6}$
   $+ \frac{5}{9}$
   _____

6. $\frac{7}{9}$
   $+ \frac{5}{18}$
   _____

7. $\frac{1}{2}$
   $+ \frac{8}{9}$
   _____

8. $\frac{6}{11}$
   $+ \frac{1}{2}$
   _____

9. $\frac{8}{9}$
   $+ \frac{4}{6}$
   _____

10. $\frac{5}{7}$
   $+ \frac{2}{3}$
   _____

◆ Find the area., ☐ = 1 square unit. Give your answers in square units.

11.

12.

13.

14.

◆ Multiply.

15. 356
   x   9

16. 7,023
   x   86

17. 53,399
   x   724

18. 1,937
   x   54

19. 447
   x 38

20. 7,369
   x 402

21. 8,623
   x 236

Bonus Box:
You get to decide how to organize the numbers 1 to 25.

22. 5,555
   x 678

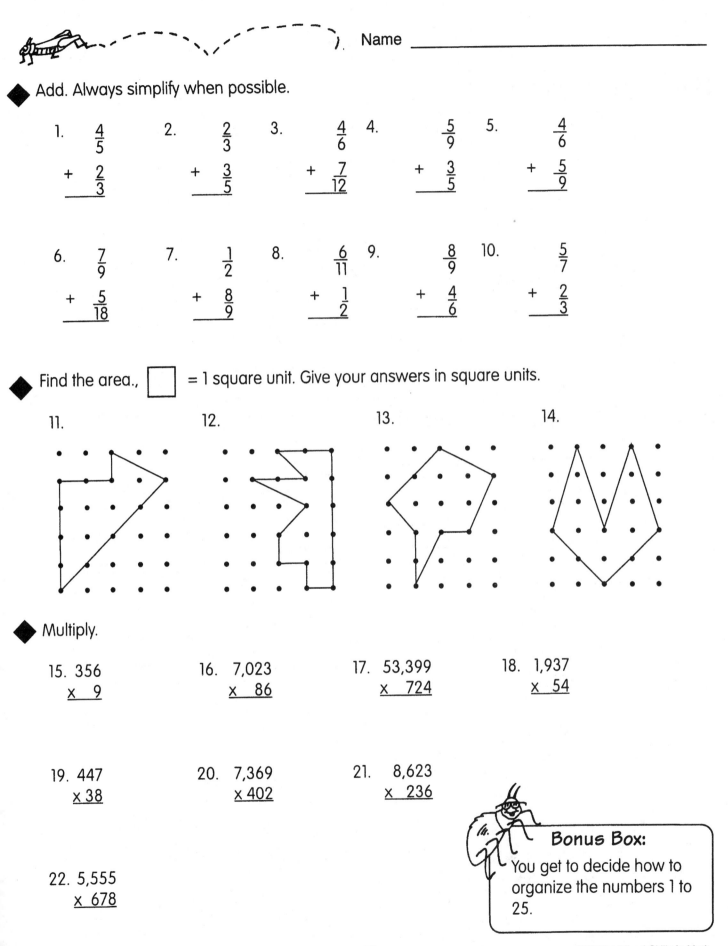

Name _____

◆ Add. Always simplify when possible.

1. $2\frac{1}{3}$ 2. $4\frac{5}{6}$ 3. $5\frac{7}{8}$ 4. $4\frac{4}{7}$ 5. $3\frac{3}{4}$

   $+ 1\frac{5}{6}$ $+ 2\frac{2}{3}$ $+ 1\frac{2}{5}$ $+ 8\frac{2}{3}$ $+ 4\frac{3}{8}$

6. $7\frac{3}{4}$ 7. $4\frac{8}{9}$ 8. $7\frac{4}{7}$ 9. $3\frac{5}{6}$ 10. $2\frac{2}{4}$

   $+ 2\frac{5}{6}$ $+ 2\frac{2}{7}$ $+ 4\frac{5}{6}$ $+ 9\frac{1}{3}$ $+ 4\frac{3}{5}$

◆ Draw all the lines of symmetry on each figure

11.   12.   13.

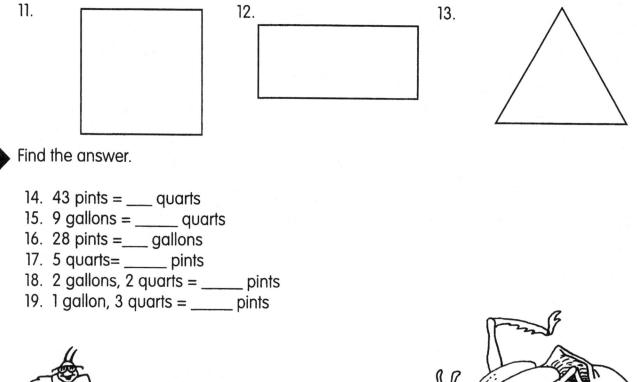

◆ Find the answer.

14. 43 pints = ____ quarts
15. 9 gallons = _____ quarts
16. 28 pints = ____ gallons
17. 5 quarts = _____ pints
18. 2 gallons, 2 quarts = _____ pints
19. 1 gallon, 3 quarts = _____ pints

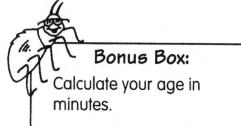

Bonus Box:
Calculate your age in
minutes.

Name _____

◆ Add. Always simplify when possible.

1. $\frac{1}{6}$
    $\frac{2}{6}$
  $+\frac{2}{6}$

2. $\frac{1}{5}$
    $\frac{1}{5}$
  $+\frac{2}{5}$

3. $\frac{3}{11}$
    $\frac{2}{11}$
  $+\frac{4}{11}$

4. $\frac{3}{16}$
    $\frac{2}{16}$
  $+\frac{7}{16}$

5. $\frac{2}{9}$
    $\frac{2}{9}$
  $+\frac{2}{9}$

6. $\frac{2}{18}$
    $\frac{5}{18}$
  $+\frac{9}{18}$

7. $\frac{3}{12}$
    $\frac{4}{12}$
  $+\frac{3}{12}$

8. $\frac{2}{15}$
    $\frac{6}{15}$
  $+\frac{4}{15}$

9. $\frac{4}{21}$
    $\frac{5}{21}$
  $+\frac{6}{21}$

10. $\frac{1}{8}$
    $\frac{3}{8}$
  $+\frac{2}{8}$

◆ Find the volume.

11.

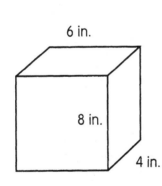

6 in.
8 in.
4 in.

12.

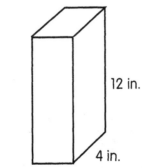

2 in.
12 in.
4 in.

13.

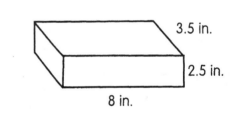

3.5 in.
2.5 in.
8 in.

◆ Divide.

14. $9\overline{)708}$ 15. $25\overline{)590}$ 16. $102\overline{)865}$ 17. $12\overline{)613}$

18. $999\overline{)8,736}$ 19. $19\overline{)87}$ 20. $74\overline{)4,003}$

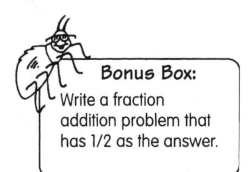

Bonus Box:
Write a fraction addition problem that has 1/2 as the answer.

21. $82\overline{)179}$

◆ Add. Always simplify when possible.

1. $\frac{3}{5}$ 2. $\frac{2}{6}$ 3. $\frac{4}{16}$ 4. $\frac{3}{8}$ 5. $\frac{4}{5}$

$\frac{3}{5}$ $\frac{3}{6}$ $\frac{6}{16}$ $\frac{6}{8}$ $\frac{3}{5}$

$+\ \frac{3}{5}$ $+\ \frac{4}{6}$ $+\ \frac{7}{16}$ $+\ \frac{5}{8}$ $+\ \frac{4}{5}$

6. $\frac{4}{10}$ 7. $\frac{3}{18}$ 8. $\frac{5}{6}$ 9. $\frac{6}{25}$ 10. $\frac{11}{20}$

$\frac{7}{10}$ $\frac{11}{18}$ $\frac{4}{6}$ $\frac{12}{25}$ $\frac{8}{20}$

$+\ \frac{6}{10}$ $+\ \frac{9}{18}$ $+\ \frac{5}{6}$ $+\ \frac{11}{25}$ $+\ \frac{7}{20}$

◆ Draw shapes with straight sides that have the perimeter requested. —— = 1 unit. Mark the units on each side.

11. 18 units   12. 30 units   13. 24 units

◆ Add or subtract.

14. 456   15. 5,836   16. 2,367   17. 20,003   18. 9,193
    762   - 3,795   - 1,983   - 9999   90,225
    67   238
    +804   +5,263

19. 2,000   20. 192,837
    - 1,937   + 564,738

Bonus Box:
Figure out and write the year in which you will turn 50.

◆ Add. Always simplify when possible.

1. $\dfrac{1}{3}$ $\dfrac{2}{5}$ $+\dfrac{1}{10}$

2. $\dfrac{1}{4}$ $\dfrac{2}{12}$ $+\dfrac{1}{3}$

3. $\dfrac{1}{5}$ $\dfrac{1}{4}$ $+\dfrac{1}{10}$

4. $\dfrac{2}{7}$ $\dfrac{1}{3}$ $+\dfrac{1}{6}$

5. $\dfrac{2}{9}$ $\dfrac{1}{3}$ $+\dfrac{1}{6}$

6. $\dfrac{2}{10}$ $\dfrac{1}{5}$ $+\dfrac{1}{2}$

7. $\dfrac{1}{8}$ $\dfrac{1}{2}$ $+\dfrac{1}{6}$

8. $\dfrac{2}{11}$ $\dfrac{1}{4}$ $+\dfrac{1}{2}$

9. $\dfrac{1}{5}$ $\dfrac{1}{2}$ $+\dfrac{1}{8}$

10. $\dfrac{1}{3}$ $\dfrac{1}{10}$ $+\dfrac{1}{2}$

◆ Remember the order of operations.

11. $(2 \times 3) + 4 \div 2 =$

12. $75 \div 3 \div 5 + 1 =$

13. $33 \times 3 + 1 \div 2 =$

14. $85 \times (7 + 3) \div 5 =$

15. $3 + (21 \div 3) \times 2 =$

16. $4 \times 2 + 5 \times 8 - 2 =$

17. $93 + (24 \div 6) - 4 \div 4 =$

18. $19 - 2 + (34 \div 2) =$

19. $9 \times 6 + (3 \times 2) =$

◆ Write three sets of coins to equal each amount.

20. 50¢   21.   75¢   22.   60¢   23.   80¢

Bonus Box:
Create a number pattern
for a classmate to solve.

Name _____

◆ Add. Always simplify when possible.

1. $\frac{1}{9}$ 2. $\frac{2}{16}$ 3. $\frac{1}{7}$ 4. $\frac{1}{10}$ 5. $\frac{1}{15}$
    $\frac{1}{4}$ $\frac{1}{2}$ $\frac{1}{21}$ $\frac{1}{15}$ $\frac{1}{4}$
  $+\frac{1}{2}$ $+\frac{1}{8}$ $+\frac{1}{3}$ $+\frac{1}{2}$ $+\frac{1}{3}$

6. $\frac{1}{9}$ 7. $\frac{1}{3}$ 8. $\frac{1}{20}$ 9. $\frac{2}{14}$ 10. $\frac{1}{12}$
    $\frac{1}{7}$ $\frac{1}{8}$ $\frac{1}{10}$ $\frac{1}{4}$ $\frac{1}{6}$
  $+\frac{1}{2}$ $+\frac{3}{12}$ $+\frac{1}{15}$ $+\frac{1}{7}$ $+\frac{1}{5}$

◆ For each shape, draw a congruent shape.

11. 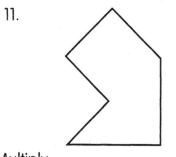   12. 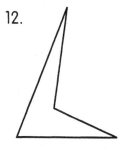   13.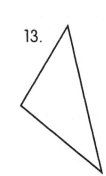

◆ Multiply.

14.   .38   15.   2.08   16.   .318   17.   43.9   18.   7.65
     x 1.7   x 1.17   x 64.4   x 6.8   x .172

19.   3.042   20.   .304
     x 34.6   x 5.63

Bonus Box:
Calculate the area of your classroom door in square inches.

21.   9.67
     x 3.49

Name _____

◆ Add. Always simplify when possible.

1. $\frac{2}{4}$ 2. $\frac{3}{8}$ 3. $\frac{3}{7}$ 4. $\frac{5}{6}$ 5. $\frac{2}{5}$
   $\frac{2}{3}$ $\frac{4}{5}$ $\frac{2}{3}$ $\frac{2}{9}$ $\frac{3}{10}$
$+\frac{5}{6}$ $+\frac{1}{2}$ $+\frac{4}{9}$ $+\frac{1}{2}$ $+\frac{7}{15}$
_____   _____   _____   _____   _____

6. $\frac{5}{6}$ 7. $\frac{4}{7}$ 8. $\frac{3}{8}$ 9. $\frac{8}{11}$ 10. $\frac{3}{4}$
   $\frac{3}{12}$ $\frac{2}{3}$ $\frac{5}{6}$ $\frac{1}{4}$ $\frac{3}{8}$
$+\frac{3}{8}$ $+\frac{6}{21}$ $+\frac{1}{3}$ $+\frac{1}{2}$ $+\frac{3}{9}$
_____   _____   _____   _____   _____

◆ Find the area. ☐ = 1 square unit. Give your answers in square units.

11.   12.   13.   14.

_____   _____   _____   _____

◆ Complete the following sentences.
   15. How many decades are in one century? _____

   16. How many days are in one decade? (Use no leap years.) _____

   17. How many hours in one week? _____

   18. How many minutes in one day? _____

   19. What is the average number of days per month in a year? _____

   20. How many days are between Valentine's Day and St. Patrick's Day? _____

Bonus Box:
Write down the hours of sleep you get from Monday through Sunday. Then find the average.

◆ Add. Always simplify when possible.

1. $3\frac{2}{3}$
  $2\frac{4}{5}$
  $+\ 6\frac{1}{2}$

2. $4\frac{6}{8}$
  $3\frac{5}{12}$
  $+\ 5\frac{2}{4}$

3. $9\frac{3}{5}$
  $4\frac{6}{10}$
  $+\ 1\frac{1}{2}$

4. $5\frac{5}{7}$
  $3\frac{3}{4}$
  $+\ 8\frac{1}{2}$

5. $4\frac{7}{8}$
  $5\frac{1}{2}$
  $+\ 3\frac{1}{4}$

6. $7\frac{3}{4}$
  $4\frac{1}{6}$
  $+\ 5\frac{7}{12}$

7. $2\frac{1}{3}$
  $3\frac{4}{7}$
  $+\ 2\frac{4}{9}$

8. $5\frac{3}{7}$
  $2\frac{3}{5}$
  $+\ 1\frac{1}{10}$

9. $3\frac{5}{6}$
  $5\frac{4}{11}$
  $+\ 2\frac{1}{2}$

10. $4\frac{4}{9}$
  $6\frac{3}{8}$
  $+\ 6\frac{1}{2}$

◆ Use a tree diagram to show the prime factors of each number.

11. 168

12. 100

13. 200

◆ Divide. If you need to extend your problem, go only one decimal place.

14. $.9\overline{)3.06}$

15. $1.4\overline{).997}$

16. $.15\overline{)590.6}$

17. $.54\overline{)1.77}$

18. $8.4\overline{).009}$

19. $53.5\overline{)100.9}$

20. $6.2\overline{)124.7}$

Bonus Box:
Estimate the length of the
hallway outside your
classroom. Then measure it.

21. $7.3\overline{)40.67}$

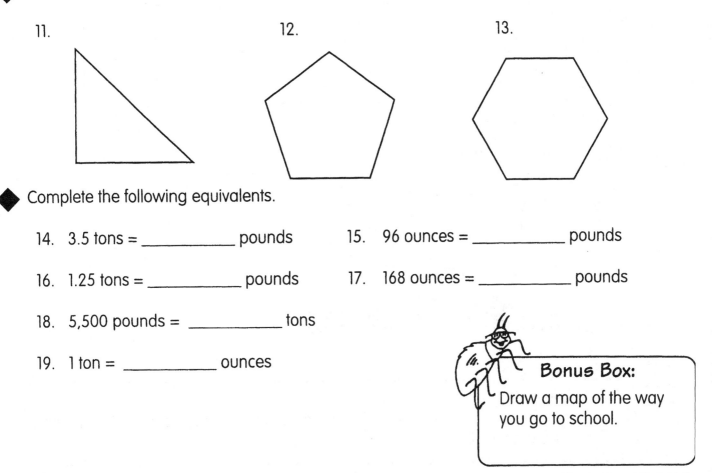

Name _____

◆ Add. Always simplify when possible.

1. $3\frac{2}{3}$ 2. $2\frac{4}{9}$ 3. $5\frac{4}{20}$ 4. $4\frac{3}{9}$ 5. $2\frac{2}{3}$

$2\frac{1}{5}$ $6\frac{2}{8}$ $4\frac{2}{6}$ $3\frac{3}{4}$ $1\frac{2}{5}$

$+\ 1\frac{1}{4}$ $+\ 7\frac{4}{6}$ $+\ 1\frac{1}{3}$ $+\ 2\frac{1}{2}$ $+\ 4\frac{3}{10}$
_____   _____   _____   _____   _____

6. $8\frac{1}{2}$ 7. $3\frac{2}{13}$ 8. $1\frac{1}{10}$ 9. $7\frac{3}{5}$ 10. $4\frac{7}{8}$

$1\frac{1}{5}$ $9\frac{1}{2}$ $4\frac{3}{5}$ $5\frac{2}{9}$ $8\frac{4}{7}$

$+\ 5\frac{9}{10}$ $+\ 2\frac{1}{3}$ $+\ 8\frac{1}{2}$ $+\ 9\frac{1}{3}$ $+\ 9\frac{1}{2}$
_____   _____   _____   _____   _____

◆ Draw the lines of symmetry on each figure.

11.   12.   13.

◆ Complete the following equivalents.

14. 3.5 tons = _____ pounds   15. 96 ounces = _____ pounds

16. 1.25 tons = _____ pounds   17. 168 ounces = _____ pounds

18. 5,500 pounds = _____ tons

19. 1 ton = _____ ounces

Bonus Box:
Draw a map of the way
you go to school.

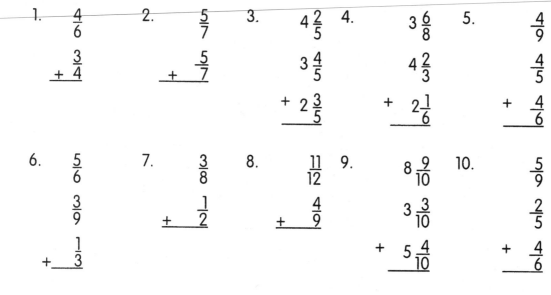

Name _____

◆ Add. Always simplify when possible.

1. $\dfrac{4}{6}$ 2. $\dfrac{5}{7}$ 3. $4\dfrac{2}{5}$ 4. $3\dfrac{6}{8}$ 5. $\dfrac{4}{9}$

$+\dfrac{3}{4}$ $+\dfrac{5}{7}$ $3\dfrac{4}{5}$ $4\dfrac{2}{3}$ $\dfrac{4}{5}$

              $+2\dfrac{3}{5}$ $+2\dfrac{1}{6}$ $+\dfrac{4}{6}$

6. $\dfrac{5}{6}$ 7. $\dfrac{3}{8}$ 8. $\dfrac{11}{12}$ 9. $8\dfrac{9}{10}$ 10. $\dfrac{5}{9}$

$\dfrac{3}{9}$ $+\dfrac{1}{2}$ $+\dfrac{4}{9}$ $3\dfrac{3}{10}$ $\dfrac{2}{5}$

$+\dfrac{1}{3}$ $+5\dfrac{4}{10}$ $+\dfrac{4}{6}$

◆ What is the capacity of each shape?

11.
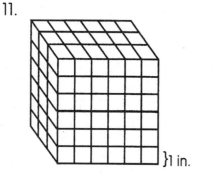
}1 in.

12.
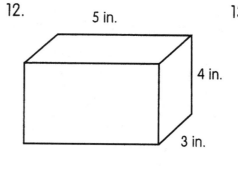
5 in.
4 in.
3 in.

13.
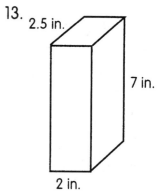
2.5 in.
7 in.
2 in.

◆ Draw the next shape in each pattern.

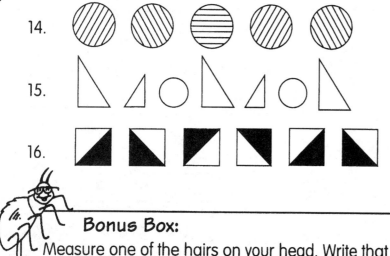

14.

15.

16.

◆ Add. Always simplify when possible.

1. $\frac{4}{5}$ 2. $5\frac{2}{3}$ 3. $3\frac{8}{10}$ 4. $\frac{6}{8}$ 5. $2\frac{1}{2}$

$\frac{2}{3}$ $+\ 4\frac{1}{9}$ $+\ 6\frac{6}{10}$ $\frac{5}{8}$ $1\frac{2}{5}$

$+\ \frac{3}{9}$ $+\ \frac{7}{8}$ $+\ 3\frac{6}{10}$

6. $\frac{8}{9}$ 7. $8\frac{5}{8}$ 8. $2\frac{3}{12}$ 9. $\frac{3}{4}$ 10. $4\frac{3}{4}$

$\frac{6}{8}$ $4\frac{4}{6}$ $1\frac{3}{4}$ $\frac{3}{4}$ $3\frac{6}{7}$

$+\ \frac{2}{3}$ $+\ 6\frac{2}{9}$ $+\ 1\frac{3}{4}$ $+\ \frac{3}{4}$ $+\ 5\frac{1}{2}$

◆ Solve.

11. $(4 \times 5) - 6 \times 3 + 5 =$ 12. $44 \div 2 + 6 \times (2 + 3) =$

13. $4 + (10 \div 2) - 7 =$ 14. $26 \div 2 \times (4 \times 3) =$

15. $(8 + 3) \times (17 - 12) =$ 16. $4 \times 3 - (6 \div 2) + 5 =$

◆ Complete the following equivalents.

17. 1 mile = _____ feet

18. 3 yards, 72 inches = _____ feet

19. 102 inches = _____ feet

20. 6 feet, 2 yards = _____ inches

21. 6 yards, 6 feet, 6 inches = _____ inches

Bonus Box:
Draw a map of the route you take to your classes each day.

◆ Subtract. Always simplify when possible.

1. $\frac{7}{8}$
    $-\frac{5}{8}$

2. $\frac{5}{9}$
    $-\frac{2}{9}$

3. $\frac{6}{7}$
    $-\frac{3}{7}$

4. $\frac{7}{10}$
    $-\frac{3}{10}$

5. $\frac{3}{4}$
    $-\frac{1}{4}$

6. $\frac{4}{11}$
    $-\frac{3}{11}$

7. $\frac{5}{6}$
    $-\frac{3}{6}$

8. $\frac{11}{12}$
    $-\frac{7}{12}$

9. $\frac{8}{15}$
    $-\frac{3}{15}$

10. $\frac{6}{9}$
    $-\frac{4}{9}$

◆ Simplify.

11. $\frac{4}{8}$

12. $\frac{7}{14}$

13. $\frac{6}{8}$

14. $\frac{10}{15}$

15. $\frac{4}{6}$

16. $\frac{9}{15}$

17. $\frac{8}{20}$

18. $\frac{2}{4}$

19. $\frac{15}{25}$

20. $\frac{8}{10}$

21. $\frac{16}{24}$

22. $\frac{25}{100}$

◆ Complete the following story problems.

23. The frozen dinner gives these directions for using the microwave. Heat for 3 minutes 30 seconds. Rotate dinner halfway through. After how much heating time should you rotate the dinner? _____

24. If you set your alarm clock for 6:15 instead of 6:00, how much extra sleep will you get over one week? _____

25. If you are to take medicine three times a day and you take the first dose at 6 AM., when should you take the other doses? _____

Bonus Box:
Write a story problem that has 76 as the answer. You can use addition, subtraction, multiplication, or division.

◆ Subtract. Always simplify when possible.

1. 7
    $-\dfrac{1}{2}$

2. 8
    $-\dfrac{3}{4}$

3. 4
    $-\dfrac{7}{12}$

4. 9
    $-\dfrac{3}{5}$

5. 8
    $-\dfrac{5}{9}$

6. 10
    $-\dfrac{7}{21}$

7. 3
    $-\dfrac{6}{8}$

8. 14
    $-\dfrac{3}{9}$

9. 5
    $-\dfrac{11}{15}$

10. 8
     $-\dfrac{7}{8}$

◆ Simplify.

11. $\dfrac{11}{8}$

12. $\dfrac{5}{3}$

13. $\dfrac{17}{15}$

14. $\dfrac{9}{6}$

15. $\dfrac{14}{4}$

16. $\dfrac{8}{3}$

17. $\dfrac{5}{2}$

18. $\dfrac{7}{3}$

19. $\dfrac{20}{5}$

20. $\dfrac{17}{6}$

21. $\dfrac{19}{4}$

22. $\dfrac{7}{3}$

◆ Determine the following equivalents.

23. 76 ounces= ——— cups

24. 3 cups = ——— ounces

25. 18 pints= ——— cups

26. 80 ounces= ——— pints

27. 1 quart = ——— ounces

28. 2 quarts = ——— pints

Bonus Box:

If you are in a group with three other people and everyone shakes hands with the others just once, how many handshakes will there be? Show how you arrived at your answer.

Name _____

◆ Subtract the following fractions. Always simplify when possible.

1. 12
    - 2
    ─────
      10

2. 8
    - 5
    ─────
      19

3. 5
    - 8
    ─────
      24

4. 15
    - 5
    ─────
      30

5. 7
    - 9
    ─────
      12

6. 32
    - 9
    ─────
      24

7. 3
    - 4
    ─────
      12

8. 10
    - 5
    ─────
      12

9. 1
    - 4
    ─────
      6

10. 4
    - 12
    ─────
      16

◆ Find the volume.

11. 1 cu. foot = _____ cu. inches

12. 1 cu. yard = _____ cu. feet

13. 2,592 cu. inches = _____ cu. feet

14. 81 cu. feet = _____ cu. yards

15. 1 cu. yard = _____ cu. inches

16. 5,184 cu. inches = _____ cu. feet

◆ Multiply.

17. 326
     x 45

18. 906
     x 48

19.   89
     x 7

20. 5,376
     x 435

21. 999
     x 88

22. 428
     x 26

23. 780
     x 60

24. 7,584
     x 576

Bonus Box:
Create drawings and examples to show a younger student who is having trouble understanding multiplication that 2 x 5 is the same as 5 x 2.

◆ Add the following fractions. Always simplify when possible.

1. $4\frac{1}{5}$
    $-\;\;\frac{4}{5}$

2. $6\frac{1}{9}$
    $-\;\;\frac{5}{9}$

3. $5\frac{2}{7}$
    $-\;\;\frac{6}{7}$

4. $8\frac{3}{12}$
    $-\;\;\frac{5}{12}$

5. $3\frac{2}{9}$
    $-\;\;\frac{8}{9}$

6. $4\frac{3}{15}$
    $-\;\;\frac{8}{15}$

7. $5\frac{3}{10}$
    $-\;\;\frac{8}{10}$

8. $9\frac{1}{8}$
    $-\;\;\frac{7}{8}$

9. $3\frac{6}{18}$
    $-\;\;\frac{10}{18}$

10. $1\frac{3}{5}$
    $-\;\;\frac{4}{5}$

◆ Solve.

11. $3^2 \times 2^2 =$

12. $5^2 \times 2 =$

13. $6^3 - 4^2 =$

14. $9^2 - 8^2 =$

15. $5^3 \div 3 =$

16. $6^2 \div 9 =$

17. $10^2 \div 5 =$

18. $65 - 7^2 =$

19. $7^2 - 3^2 =$

◆ Give the correct change and possible bills and coins to make the change.

20. $3.79 paid for with $5 bill.

21. $18.76 paid for with $20 bill.

22. $6.23 paid for with seven $1 bills.

Bonus Box:
Write a problem using exponents for a class-mate to solve.

Name _____

◆ Subtract the following fractions. Always simplify when possible.

1. $5\frac{1}{7}$
   $- 2\frac{6}{7}$

2. $7\frac{3}{8}$
   $- 4\frac{7}{8}$

3. $9\frac{3}{10}$
   $- 5\frac{7}{10}$

4. $7\frac{2}{5}$
   $- 6\frac{4}{5}$

5. $8\frac{3}{9}$
   $- 5\frac{7}{9}$

6. $10\frac{6}{15}$
   $- 4\frac{13}{15}$

7. $8\frac{2}{16}$
   $- 5\frac{15}{16}$

8. $3\frac{1}{15}$
   $- 1\frac{13}{15}$

9. $6\frac{2}{14}$
   $- 4\frac{9}{14}$

10. $9\frac{3}{8}$
    $- 8\frac{7}{8}$

◆ Find the area. ▢ = 1 square unit.

11.

12.

13.

14.

◆ Add.

15.   46
      835
    8,294
  +90,234

16.   426
        92
     3,285
   +   8

17. 91,274
   +83,640

18.   476
      927
      772
    + 338

19. 37,482
   + 39,681

50

Bonus Box:
Write a code and a message in that code for a classmate to solve.

◆ Subtract. Always simplify when possible.

1. $\dfrac{6}{8}$ $-\dfrac{1}{3}$

2. $\dfrac{7}{9}$ $-\dfrac{1}{4}$

3. $\dfrac{14}{15}$ $-\dfrac{4}{10}$

4. $\dfrac{23}{25}$ $-\dfrac{2}{5}$

5. $\dfrac{5}{6}$ $-\dfrac{1}{3}$

6. $\dfrac{6}{7}$ $-\dfrac{1}{2}$

7. $\dfrac{15}{16}$ $-\dfrac{1}{8}$

8. $\dfrac{11}{13}$ $-\dfrac{1}{3}$

9. $\dfrac{4}{5}$ $-\dfrac{3}{10}$

10. $\dfrac{2}{3}$ $-\dfrac{1}{4}$

◆ Fill in the shape that comes next in each pattern.

11. $\sqsubset \sqcap \sqcup \sqcup \sqsubset \sqcap \sqcup$

12. $< \ > \lor \land < \ >$

13. (spiral pattern)

14. (square pattern)

◆ Solve the following problems. Remember the order of operations.

15. $(6 - 3) + 8 \div 2 =$

16. $5 \times (8 + 4) \div 6 + 3 =$

17. $4 \times 9 - (4 \times 2) =$

18. $5 - 2 + (8 \div 2) \times 3 =$

19. $11 - 5 + 4 \div 2 =$

20. $(8 \times 4) - (4 \times 4) + 4 =$

Bonus Box:
Draw a shape that has straight line borders and a perimeter of 12 inches. Use actual inches to draw and measure.

◆ Subtract. Always simplify when possible.

1. $\dfrac{1}{4}$ $-\dfrac{13}{100}$ 2. $\dfrac{3}{4}$ $-\dfrac{7}{20}$ 3. $\dfrac{7}{9}$ $-\dfrac{1}{6}$ 4. $\dfrac{6}{7}$ $-\dfrac{3}{5}$ 5. $\dfrac{5}{6}$ $-\dfrac{1}{2}$

6. $\dfrac{13}{15}$ $-\dfrac{7}{10}$ 7. $\dfrac{9}{10}$ $-\dfrac{3}{6}$ 8. $\dfrac{7}{8}$ $-\dfrac{2}{5}$ 9. $\dfrac{4}{5}$ $-\dfrac{4}{7}$ 10. $\dfrac{11}{12}$ $-\dfrac{5}{6}$

◆ Draw shapes with straight sides that have the perimeter requested. ¼ inch = 1 unit. Mark the units on each side and fit in the space allowed.

11. 12 units

12. 20 units

13. 28 units

◆ Multiply.

14. 5.03
     x .07

15. 56.9
     x 4.03

16. 4.132
     x .008

17. 2.67
     x 89

18. 67.2
     x .64

19. 5.3
     x 2.06

20. 8.17
     x 4.3

21. 191
     x .034

Bonus Box:

If you are standing in a group of 5 people and each person shakes hands with every other person once, how many handshakes will be given? Give your answer and reasoning.

Name _____

◆ Subtract the following fractions. Always simplify when possible.

1. $\frac{1}{5}$
    $-\frac{19}{100}$

2. $\frac{4}{6}$
    $-\frac{3}{5}$

3. $\frac{8}{9}$
    $-\frac{2}{3}$

4. $\frac{5}{7}$
    $-\frac{1}{2}$

5. $\frac{1}{3}$
    $-\frac{1}{4}$

6. $\frac{5}{8}$
    $-\frac{1}{2}$

7. $\frac{1}{2}$
    $-\frac{4}{9}$

8. $\frac{1}{3}$
    $-\frac{1}{6}$

9. $\frac{5}{9}$
    $-\frac{1}{2}$

10. $\frac{11}{12}$
    $-\frac{3}{4}$

◆ Draw the lines of symmetry.

11.

12.

13.

◆ Solve the following story problems.

14. If a brand-new pencil was eight inches long and you used up ¼ of it, how long would your pencil be then? _____

15. What fractional part of the eight-inch pencil would you have to use up to have a pencil that is two inches long? _____

16. If you walk three yards and one foot to the pencil sharpener, how far is that in feet?

_____

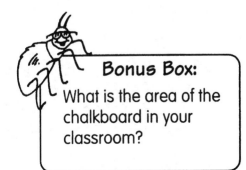

Bonus Box:
What is the area of the chalkboard in your classroom?

◆ Subtract the following fractions. Always simplify when possible.

1. $7\frac{1}{2}$
   $-\frac{7}{8}$

2. $3\frac{2}{9}$
   $-\frac{6}{8}$

3. $9\frac{1}{8}$
   $-\frac{9}{10}$

4. $5\frac{1}{10}$
   $-\frac{6}{7}$

5. $1\frac{1}{7}$
   $-\frac{2}{3}$

6. $7\frac{1}{3}$
   $-\frac{5}{6}$

7. $8\frac{1}{9}$
   $-\frac{6}{7}$

8. $2\frac{2}{5}$
   $-\frac{1}{2}$

9. $4\frac{4}{5}$
   $-\frac{8}{9}$

10. $3\frac{2}{4}$
   $-\frac{6}{9}$

◆ Solve the following problems. Remember the order of operations.

11. $(6 \times 7) + (4 \times 2) - 25 =$

12. $19 - (3^2) + 32 \div 2 =$

13. $35 + 11 - 6 \div 2 =$

14. $(21 - 6) \times (9 \div 3) + 5 =$

15. $94 - 2 + 3 - (5 \times 5) =$

16. $5 \times 6 \div 3 \div 2 \times 10 =$

◆ Add.

17. $3\frac{2}{4}$
   $+\frac{3}{4}$

18. $4\frac{6}{8}$
   $+\frac{7}{8}$

19. $2\frac{5}{6}$
   $+\frac{4}{6}$

20. $11\frac{4}{9}$
   $+\frac{7}{9}$

21. $9\frac{9}{10}$
   $+\frac{7}{10}$

22. $8\frac{6}{7}$
   $+\frac{5}{7}$

23. $3\frac{11}{12}$
   $+\frac{9}{12}$

24. $8\frac{4}{5}$
   $+\frac{3}{5}$

Bonus Box:
How many feet from the chalkboard is your desk? Change that measurement to inches. Finally, change the inches to meters.

◆ Subtract. Always simplify when possible.

1. $5\frac{2}{9}$
   $-\frac{7}{8}$

2. $2\frac{1}{10}$
   $-\frac{11}{12}$

3. $5\frac{3}{15}$
   $-\frac{4}{5}$

4. $9\frac{2}{18}$
   $-\frac{7}{9}$

5. $7\frac{3}{8}$
   $-\frac{15}{16}$

6. $1\frac{2}{3}$
   $-\frac{5}{6}$

7. $6\frac{4}{7}$
   $-\frac{9}{10}$

8. $8\frac{5}{8}$
   $-\frac{3}{4}$

9. $3\frac{4}{17}$
   $-\frac{1}{2}$

10. $9\frac{2}{9}$
    $-\frac{5}{6}$

◆ Find the volume.

11. 7 ½ in.

8 in.

3 ½ in.

12.

9 ½ in.

3 ½ in.

1 ½ in.

13. 4 in.

5 in.

7.5 in.

◆ Divide.

14. $75\overline{)169}$

15. $9\overline{)3,378}$

16. $50\overline{)498}$

17. $19\overline{)2,328}$

18. $7\overline{)483}$

19. $68\overline{)9,934}$

20. $81\overline{)9,378}$

21. $451\overline{)1,954}$

Bonus Box:

Organize the whole numbers from 1 to 50. Choose your own organization plan and be ready to explain it. You may not use putting the numbers in counting order.

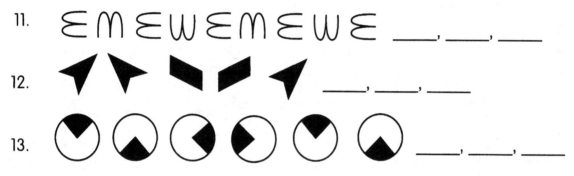

◆ Subtract. Always simplify when possible.

1. $5\frac{2}{3}$
    $-3\frac{8}{9}$

2. $12\frac{1}{9}$
    $-7\frac{5}{6}$

3. $9\frac{3}{9}$
    $-3\frac{5}{6}$

4. $7\frac{2}{12}$
    $-2\frac{7}{8}$

5. $4\frac{1}{15}$
    $-2\frac{2}{3}$

6. $5\frac{1}{13}$
    $-3\frac{1}{3}$

7. $6\frac{2}{10}$
    $-4\frac{1}{4}$

8. $8\frac{1}{7}$
    $-5\frac{2}{3}$

9. $6\frac{2}{5}$
    $-1\frac{5}{6}$

10. $1\frac{1}{6}$
    $-\frac{3}{4}$

◆ Fill in the next three shapes in each sequence.

11. Ɛ M Ɛ W Ɛ M Ɛ W Ɛ ___, ___, ___

12. ___, ___, ___

13. ___, ___, ___

◆ Solve the following story problems.

14. Shirley and Katie like to visit on the Internet. The only problem is that Shirley lives in Nebraska, and Katie lives in California. If Katie waits until 7 PM to meet Shirley, what time will it be where Shirley lives? _____

15. The hands of a clock form a right angle at 9 o'clock. List three times when the angle formed by the hands is greater than 90°. _____

Bonus Box:
Write an addition problem that has ¼ as the answer.

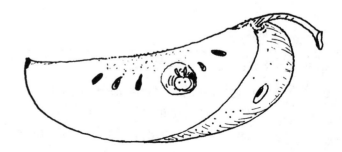

◆ Subtract. Always simplify when possible.

1. $4\frac{1}{7}$ 2. $8\frac{4}{10}$ 3. $3\frac{1}{6}$ 4. $9\frac{2}{9}$ 5. $5\frac{2}{11}$

   $-2\frac{4}{5}$ $-4\frac{7}{8}$ $-1\frac{4}{5}$ $-5\frac{5}{6}$ $-2\frac{4}{5}$

6. $10\frac{3}{15}$ 7. $11\frac{3}{16}$ 8. $4\frac{6}{25}$ 9. $3\frac{1}{5}$ 10. $7\frac{3}{8}$

   $-7\frac{8}{9}$ $-3\frac{5}{6}$ $-1\frac{9}{10}$ $-1\frac{6}{7}$ $-3\frac{6}{7}$

◆ Draw and shade in shapes that have the specified area.

11. 15 sq. units   12. 10 sq. units   13. 9 sq. units

◆ Write the equivalent measurements.

14. 1 km = _____ m

15. 64 m = _____ cm

16. 4.5 m = _____ cm

17. 995 mm = _____ cm

18. 4,500 mm = _____ m

19. 1 k = _____ cm

Bonus Box:
Mario, Sam, Gino, and Harry decided to race each other. Use diagrams or pictures to show how many different ways they could finish the race.

◆ Subtract. Always simplify when possible.

1. $4\frac{2}{9}$ 2. $\frac{9}{10}$ 3. $6\frac{1}{3}$ 4. $2\frac{1}{4}$ 5. $1\frac{2}{7}$
   $-2\frac{7}{9}$ $-\frac{4}{10}$ $-\frac{7}{8}$ $-\frac{6}{8}$ $-\frac{2}{3}$

6. $5\frac{1}{9}$ 7. $5\frac{1}{15}$ 8. $\frac{46}{50}$ 9. $3\frac{2}{8}$ 10. $\frac{98}{100}$
   $-2\frac{5}{9}$ $-1\frac{2}{3}$ $-\frac{16}{50}$ $-1\frac{7}{8}$ $-\frac{3}{4}$

◆ Continue the pattern three places.

11. 5, 15, 25, 35, 45, _____, _____, _____

12. 1, 3, 7, 15, 31, 63, _____, _____, _____

13. 1, 6, 16, 31, 51, 76, _____, _____, _____

14. 1, 7, 1, 7, 1, 7, 1, _____, _____, _____

◆ Divide.

15. $.06\overline{)9.47}$ 16. $4.1\overline{)68.3}$ 17. $.007\overline{)3.241}$ 18. $5.1\overline{)5,732}$

19. $8\overline{)34.02}$ 20. $.6\overline{)4,382}$ 21. $.32\overline{)9.678}$ 22. $5.8\overline{)56.93}$

Bonus Box:
Design a quilt square with four congruent shapes and two lines of symmetry.

◆ Subtract. Always simplify when possible.

1. $\frac{8}{9}$
   $-\frac{7}{8}$

2. $4\frac{2}{3}$
   $-2\frac{6}{8}$

3. $5\frac{2}{9}$
   $-1\frac{7}{9}$

4. $2\frac{6}{7}$
   $-\frac{3}{4}$

5. $12\frac{2}{5}$
   $-7\frac{3}{5}$

6. $4\frac{4}{5}$
   $-1\frac{3}{8}$

7. $3\frac{3}{7}$
   $-1\frac{2}{3}$

8. $9\frac{1}{2}$
   $-4\frac{5}{6}$

9. $3\frac{1}{2}$
   $-\frac{1}{3}$

10. $7\frac{3}{15}$
    $-2\frac{3}{4}$

◆ Solve the following problems. Remember order of operations.

11. $(3 \times 4) \div (4 - 2) + 4 =$

12. $75 - (5 \times 5) \div 5 =$

13. $(75 - 5) \times 5 \div 5 =$

14. $64 - 16 + 4 \div 10 =$

15. $(6 \times 7) + (3 \times 5) \div 5 =$

16. $6 \times (7 + 3) \times (5 \times 5) =$

◆ Add.

17. $\frac{5}{8}$
    $+\frac{5}{8}$

18. $\frac{3}{7}$
    $+\frac{4}{5}$

19. $\frac{4}{9}$
    $+\frac{3}{4}$

20. $\frac{6}{10}$
    $+\frac{2}{4}$

21. $4\frac{2}{3}$
    $+2\frac{1}{4}$

22. $\frac{1}{2}$
    $+\frac{5}{8}$

23. $3\frac{1}{5}$
    $+5\frac{4}{10}$

24. $5\frac{2}{5}$
    $+2\frac{6}{7}$

Bonus Box:
Write both a fraction and a decimal to show how many of the people in your class are left-handed.

◆ Subtract. Always simplify when possible.

1. $7\frac{3}{4}$
   $-5\frac{6}{7}$

2. $3\frac{1}{9}$
   $-1\frac{4}{5}$

3. $2\frac{3}{18}$
   $-\frac{5}{6}$

4. $\frac{7}{10}$
   $-\frac{3}{10}$

5. $\frac{7}{16}$
   $-\frac{1}{3}$

6. $4\frac{4}{5}$
   $-2\frac{7}{10}$

7. $2\frac{1}{8}$
   $-1\frac{5}{6}$

8. $9\frac{2}{3}$
   $-4\frac{5}{7}$

9. $4\frac{1}{9}$
   $-2\frac{2}{3}$

10. $\frac{6}{9}$
    $-\frac{1}{3}$

◆ Draw the lines of symmetry.

11.

12.

13.

◆ Solve the following story problems.

14. If you have five coins in your pocket, and they add up to 30¢, what coins might you have?
    _____

15. If you have four coins in your pocket, and they add up to 90¢, what coins might you have?
    _____

16. If you have eight coins in your pocket, and they add up to 50¢, what coins might you have?
    _____

Bonus Box:
Write a fraction to tell how many pieces of furniture out of all the pieces of furniture in your living room at home you can sit on.

◆ Multiply. Always simplify when possible.

1. $\frac{1}{3} \times \frac{2}{5} =$

2. $\frac{1}{2} \times \frac{1}{4} =$

3. $\frac{2}{3} \times \frac{1}{5} =$

4. $\frac{5}{7} \times \frac{2}{3} =$

5. $\frac{7}{8} \times \frac{3}{5} =$

6. $\frac{7}{10} \times \frac{1}{2} =$

7. $\frac{3}{4} \times \frac{1}{4} =$

8. $\frac{1}{8} \times \frac{2}{5} =$

9. $\frac{4}{7} \times \frac{2}{3} =$

10. $\frac{4}{9} \times \frac{1}{3} =$

11. $\frac{3}{7} \times \frac{2}{5} =$

12. $\frac{3}{8} \times \frac{1}{3} =$

◆ Place the decimal in the right place to make each statement reasonable.

13. Marge paid $1195 for a T-shirt.

14. Pam drives 152 miles to work each day.

15. Mary paid $395 for a sandwich.

16. Michael weighed 235 pounds as a three-year-old.

17. The movie ticket cost $450 and the popcorn cost $275.

◆ Add or subtract.

18. $3\frac{4}{5}$
    $- 1\frac{5}{6}$

19. $8\frac{7}{8}$
    $- 1\frac{3}{4}$

20. $5\frac{2}{3}$
    $- 3\frac{5}{9}$

21. $\frac{4}{6}$
    $+ \frac{4}{8}$

22. $5\frac{1}{9}$
    $- 2\frac{7}{8}$

23. $4\frac{2}{7}$
    $- 1\frac{5}{6}$

24. $1\frac{4}{5}$
    $+ 3\frac{2}{3}$

25. $\frac{8}{11}$
    $+ \frac{1}{4}$

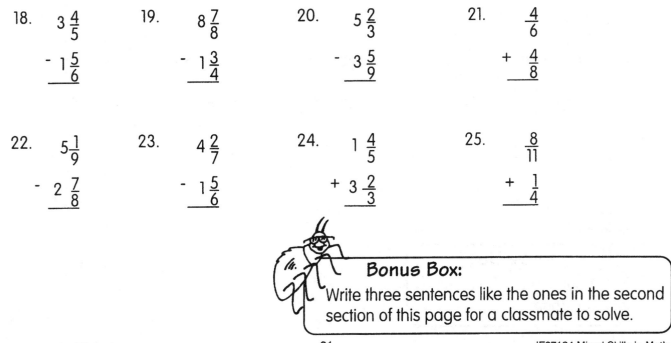

Bonus Box:
Write three sentences like the ones in the second section of this page for a classmate to solve.

Name _____

◆ Multiply. Always simplify when possible.

1. $\frac{7}{8} \times \frac{5}{10} =$ 2. $\frac{8}{11} \times \frac{3}{5} =$ 3. $\frac{5}{11} \times \frac{1}{4} =$

4. $\frac{1}{8} \times \frac{3}{7} =$ 5. $\frac{2}{3} \times \frac{1}{9} =$ 6. $\frac{5}{6} \times \frac{5}{7} =$

7. $\frac{4}{5} \times \frac{4}{7} =$ 8. $\frac{2}{9} \times \frac{4}{5} =$ 9. $\frac{4}{9} \times \frac{2}{9} =$

10. $\frac{1}{3} \times \frac{2}{4} =$ 11. $\frac{5}{8} \times \frac{3}{4} =$ 12. $\frac{6}{7} \times \frac{1}{5} =$

◆ What is the most likely temperature for:

13.	ice cream	6°C	-2°C	-35°C
14.	ice skating outside	-3°C	35°C	100°C
15.	playing softball	5°C	25°C	75°C
16.	a cup of hot coffee	40°C	80°C	180°C

◆ Find the average.

17. 5, 8, 6, 7, 5, 3, 4, 6   18. 6, 4, 5, 8, 7, 6, 2, 0,

19. 70, 74, 75, 79, 78, 77   20. 78, 79, 78, 76, 75, 65

21. 98, 97, 98, 95, 94, 97   22. 85, 88, 84, 86, 88, 75

Bonus Box:
Draw a map of your classroom.

Name _____

◆ Multiply. Always simplify when possible.

1. $\frac{2}{3} \times \frac{1}{2} =$

2. $\frac{2}{3} \times \frac{5}{10} =$

3. $\frac{6}{11} \times \frac{1}{3} =$

4. $\frac{5}{9} \times 3 =$

5. $4 \times \frac{6}{8} =$

6. $\frac{5}{6} \times \frac{3}{4} =$

7. $\frac{8}{10} \times \frac{1}{4} =$

8. $\frac{3}{15} \times \frac{3}{6} =$

9. $\frac{2}{3} \times \frac{9}{10} =$

10. $\frac{2}{14} \times \frac{7}{10} =$

11. $\frac{5}{6} \times \frac{5}{10} =$

12. $\frac{2}{3} \times \frac{3}{8} =$

◆ Write three other fractions that are equivalent to the given fraction. Be certain to include the simplest form of the fraction.

13. $\frac{25}{100}$ _____, _____, _____

16. $\frac{12}{24}$ _____, _____, _____

14. $\frac{12}{18}$ _____, _____, _____

17. $\frac{20}{60}$ _____, _____, _____

15. $\frac{24}{36}$ _____, _____, _____

◆ Divide.

18. $8\overline{)495}$

19. $53\overline{)4,958}$

20. $.08\overline{)3.95}$

21. $.31\overline{)845}$

22. $9\overline{)2,764}$

23. $.003\overline{)34.8}$

24. $75\overline{).0065}$

25. $5.2\overline{)82.9}$

Bonus Box:
Average the grades you have gotten so far in this class.

◆ Multiply. Always simplify when possible.

1. $\frac{6}{14} \times \frac{6}{10} =$

2. $\frac{1}{4} \times \frac{5}{8} =$

3. $3 \times \frac{2}{9} =$

4. $\frac{2}{4} \times \frac{5}{6} =$

5. $6 \times \frac{1}{3} =$

6. $\frac{1}{10} \times 100 =$

7. $\frac{7}{25} \times \frac{5}{14} =$

8. $\frac{3}{4} \times \frac{4}{5} =$

9. $\frac{3}{4} \times \frac{2}{5} =$

10. $\frac{8}{10} \times \frac{2}{4} =$

11. $\frac{21}{22} \times \frac{2}{3} =$

12. $\frac{3}{10} \times \frac{5}{6} =$

◆ Write the following equivalents.

13. 3 minutes = ————— seconds

14. 2.5 hours = ————— minutes

15. 14 days = ————— weeks

16. 3.5 days = ————— hours

17. 730 days = ————— years

18. 150 years = ——— centuries

19. 36 hours = ————— days

20. 180 minutes = ——— hours

◆ Round the following numbers to the places specified.

21. Round 54,093,267 to the ten thousands place _____

22. Round 5,395,339 to the hundreds place _____

23. Round 12,736.93748 to the thousands place _____

24. Round 56,395.66826 to the ten thousandths place _____

Bonus Box:
Write a fraction subtraction problem that has ¼ as the answer.

◆ Multiply. Always simplify when possible.

1. $7\frac{3}{10} \times 6\frac{1}{4} =$

2. $4\frac{1}{3} \times 9\frac{5}{8} =$

3. $6\frac{2}{3} \times 3\frac{5}{6} =$

4. $4\frac{4}{9} \times 2\frac{3}{8} =$

5. $7\frac{1}{8} \times 3\frac{2}{3} =$

6. $4\frac{4}{5} \times 2\frac{3}{8} =$

7. $3\frac{3}{4} \times 4\frac{8}{9} =$

8. $4\frac{2}{3} \times 4\frac{3}{4} =$

9. $8\frac{2}{7} \times 3\frac{7}{8} =$

10. $3\frac{2}{5} \times 6\frac{10}{12} =$

11. $5\frac{1}{5} \times 8\frac{3}{4} =$

12. $7\frac{3}{5} \times 3\frac{2}{4} =$

◆ Draw the lines of symmetry.

13.

14.

15.

◆ Add or subtract.

16. 83,349
   +11,357

17. 837
   -249

18. 5,338
   +2,997

19. 50,002
   -39,876

20. 40,603
   - 6,538

21. 902
   +178

22. 2,000
   -1,937

23. 2,025
   +1,634

Bonus Box:
What is the approximate area of the chair seat you use in this class?

◆ Multiply. Always simplify when possible.

1. $4\frac{3}{5} \times 2\frac{2}{3} =$

2. $9\frac{3}{5} \times 3\frac{2}{5} =$

3. $5\frac{6}{7} \times 3\frac{7}{9} =$

4. $2\frac{5}{12} \times 6\frac{1}{3} =$

5. $4\frac{3}{8} \times 6\frac{4}{5} =$

6. $8\frac{5}{6} \times 5\frac{7}{10} =$

7. $7\frac{1}{8} \times 7\frac{2}{3} =$

8. $3\frac{3}{4} \times 9\frac{5}{6} =$

9. $4\frac{3}{7} \times 4\frac{1}{4} =$

10. $8\frac{5}{6} \times 3\frac{2}{9} =$

11. $9\frac{8}{9} \times 5\frac{1}{3} =$

12. $4\frac{2}{5} \times 2\frac{3}{4} =$

◆ Make a tree diagram to factor these numbers to their primes.

13. 296

14. 148

15. 70

◆ Multiply.

16.   43.6
    $\times$ 2.8

17.   9,983
    $\times$ .0032

18.   4.253
    $\times$ 1.3

19.   537
    $\times$ 84

20.   95
    $\times$ 28

21.   565
    $\times$ 432

22. 5,009
    $\times$ 3.02

23.   56.2
    $\times$ 2.3

Bonus Box:
Instead of numbers, use shapes to make a pattern for a classmate to figure out and add the next three shapes.

Name _____

◆ Multiply. Always simplify when possible.

1. $\frac{4}{7} \times \frac{1}{2} =$

2. $3\frac{3}{4} \times \frac{6}{8} =$

3. $8 \times \frac{2}{3} =$

4. $\frac{11}{12} \times 6\frac{6}{8} =$

5. $\frac{4}{5} \times 9\frac{2}{3} =$

6. $\frac{3}{4} \times 8 =$

7. $\frac{5}{9} \times \frac{6}{7} =$

8. $\frac{2}{4} \times \frac{4}{8} =$

9. $5 \times \frac{4}{5} =$

10. $\frac{3}{6} \times 5\frac{2}{3} =$

11. $8\frac{5}{6} \times 3\frac{1}{3} =$

12. $5\frac{2}{5} \times 5\frac{5}{6} =$

◆ Find the area. ▢ = 1 square unit

13.   14.   15.

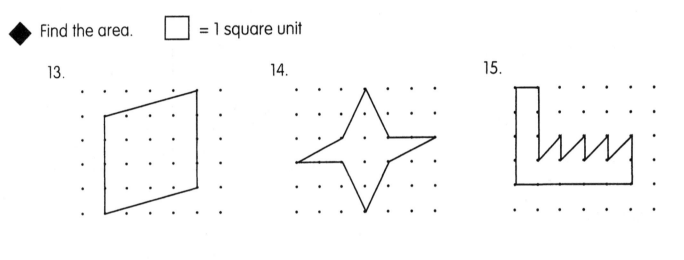

◆ What is the smallest common multiple for these numbers?

16. 2, 3, 4 _____

17. 5, 4, 3 _____

18. 4, 7, 2 _____

19. 5, 3, 10 _____

20. 6, 9, 3 _____

21. 11, 2, 4 _____

22. 5, 2, 8 _____

23. 5, 6, 3 _____

24. 8, 6, 3 _____

Bonus Box:
Design and label a quilt square with two lines of symmetry, four congruent shapes, and two similar shapes.

Name _____

◆ Multiply. Always simplify when possible

1. $5 \times \frac{6}{10} =$

2. $8\frac{2}{3} \times 4\frac{1}{6} =$

3. $3\frac{2}{5} \times 2\frac{1}{4} =$

4. $\frac{9}{10} \times \frac{5}{6} =$

5. $\frac{6}{9} \times 5 =$

6. $\frac{3}{5} \times \frac{15}{16} =$

7. $7\frac{2}{14} \times \frac{3}{4} =$

8. $7\frac{3}{5} \times 2\frac{1}{2} =$

9. $\frac{7}{9} \times \frac{6}{7} =$

10. $8 \times \frac{4}{5} =$

11. $4\frac{2}{3} \times 7 =$

12. $\frac{4}{5} \times \frac{5}{6} =$

◆ For each angle write acute, obtuse, or right.

13. ∠COE _____

14. ∠AOE _____

15. ∠AOD _____

16. ∠EOF _____

◆ Add or subtract.

17. $\frac{3}{4}$
$+ \frac{3}{5}$

18. $\frac{5}{6}$
$- \frac{1}{3}$

19. $4\frac{1}{8}$
$- 2\frac{3}{4}$

20. $8\frac{1}{9}$
$+ 1\frac{4}{5}$

21. $\frac{8}{9}$
$+ \frac{1}{2}$

22. $3\frac{1}{7}$
$+ 2\frac{1}{8}$

23. $8\frac{3}{15}$
$- 5\frac{3}{5}$

24. $\frac{6}{7}$
$- \frac{4}{9}$

Bonus Box:

If all students in your present class shake hands with each other once, how many handshakes will that be? Give your answer and reasoning.

Name _____

◆ Always simplify when possible.

Write the reciprocal for each fraction.

1. $\frac{1}{8}$ 2. $\frac{3}{4}$ 3. $\frac{2}{5}$ 4. $\frac{2}{9}$ 5. $\frac{2}{3}$

6. $\frac{3}{7}$ 7. $\frac{4}{5}$ 8. $\frac{1}{5}$ 9. $\frac{2}{10}$ 10. $\frac{3}{8}$

◆ Write the equivalent measurements.

11. 12 ft = _____ in.

12. 7 ⅓ yd. = _____ ft.

13. 36 in. = _____ ft.

14. 13 ft. = _____ yd.

15. 111 in.= _____ yd.

16. 4 ft. 8 in. _____ in.

17. 41 ft. = _____ yd. _____ ft.

18. 10 yd. = _____ ft.

19. 3 ¼ yd = _____ ft.

20. 108 in. = _____ yd.

◆ Use this number to answer the following questions: 123,456,789.

What number is in the
21. thousands place? _____

22. ten millions place? _____

23. hundred thousands place? _____

24. tens place? _____

25. millions place? _____

26. thousands place? _____

27. ten thousands place? _____

Bonus Box:
List all the combinations of coins that you could use to pay for school lunch for one day.

◆ Divide. Always simplify when possible.

1. $\dfrac{3}{5} \div \dfrac{2}{4} =$

2. $\dfrac{4}{6} \div \dfrac{2}{3} =$

3. $4 \div \dfrac{4}{5} =$

4. $\dfrac{5}{7} \div \dfrac{1}{9} =$

5. $11 \div \dfrac{4}{6} =$

6. $\dfrac{1}{6} \div \dfrac{2}{8} =$

7. $\dfrac{4}{5} \div \dfrac{1}{3} =$

8. $\dfrac{2}{9} \div \dfrac{2}{7} =$

9. $\dfrac{3}{4} \div \dfrac{3}{5} =$

10. $\dfrac{4}{7} \div \dfrac{1}{6} =$

11. $\dfrac{3}{12} \div \dfrac{1}{3} =$

12. $\dfrac{5}{16} \div \dfrac{3}{8} =$

◆ Write the largest common factor of each group of numbers.

13. 5, 10, 15

14. 8, 6

15. 9, 6

16. 6, 8, 12

17. 18, 12, 24

18. 7, 11

19. 8, 20, 24

20. 16, 24, 12

21. 16, 24, 32

◆ Multiply.

22. $\begin{array}{r} 6.83 \\ \times\ 3.4 \\ \hline \end{array}$

23. $\begin{array}{r} 186 \\ \times\ 53 \\ \hline \end{array}$

24. $\begin{array}{r} 9.352 \\ \times\ 2.043 \\ \hline \end{array}$

25. $\begin{array}{r} 9{,}898 \\ \times\ .745 \\ \hline \end{array}$

26. $\begin{array}{r} 56.38 \\ \times\ 5.64 \\ \hline \end{array}$

27. $\begin{array}{r} 3{,}748 \\ \times\ 768 \\ \hline \end{array}$

Bonus Box:
List the distances that you and four friends live from school. Then find the average distance. Which of you lives closest to the average?

Name _____

◆ Divide. Always simplify when possible.

1. $4 \div \dfrac{7}{10} =$

2. $\dfrac{2}{3} \div \dfrac{4}{5} =$

3. $\dfrac{5}{6} \div \dfrac{4}{7} =$

4. $\dfrac{3}{8} \div \dfrac{2}{5} =$

5. $\dfrac{1}{8} \div \dfrac{8}{9} =$

6. $\dfrac{3}{5} \div \dfrac{2}{4} =$

7. $\dfrac{11}{12} \div \dfrac{5}{7} =$

8. $4 \div \dfrac{3}{5} =$

9. $\dfrac{5}{9} \div \dfrac{3}{4} =$

10. $\dfrac{4}{9} \div 5 =$

11. $\dfrac{7}{8} \div \dfrac{2}{3} =$

12. $6 \div \dfrac{5}{6} =$

◆ Write the equivalents of the measurements.

13. 5 gal. = _____ qt.

14. 6 lb = _____ oz.

15. 30 qt. = _____ gal.

16. 10 qt. = _____ gal.

17. 64 oz. = _____ lb.

18. 2 gal. = _____ pt.

19. 12 oz.= _____ lb.

20. 35 qt. = _____ gal.

21. 750 lb. = _____ ton

22. 10 fl oz. = _____ c.

23. 2 c = _____ fl. oz.

24. 25 fl oz. = ___ c. __ fl. oz.

◆ Divide.

25. $85\overline{)869}$

26. $.07\overline{)32.98}$

27. $19\overline{)4063}$

28. $1\overline{)7\ 859}$

29. $25\overline{)1.006}$

30. $30\overline{)758}$

Bonus Box:
Stack all your school books on top of each other. Measure the height in inches and in centimeters. Write your measurements.

◆ Divide. Always simplify when possible.

1. $\dfrac{2}{3} \div \dfrac{2}{6} =$

2. $\dfrac{8}{9} \div \dfrac{3}{4} =$

3. $\dfrac{4}{9} \div \dfrac{4}{6} =$

4. $\dfrac{2}{12} \div \dfrac{6}{8} =$

5. $4 \div \dfrac{8}{9} =$

6. $\dfrac{7}{8} \div \dfrac{4}{21} =$

7. $\dfrac{5}{9} \div \dfrac{10}{18} =$

8. $\dfrac{15}{16} \div \dfrac{3}{8} =$

9. $4 \div \dfrac{8}{12} =$

10. $\dfrac{6}{7} \div \dfrac{12}{21} =$

11. $15 \div \dfrac{2}{3} =$

12. $\dfrac{9}{10} \div \dfrac{3}{5} =$

◆ For each angle write acute, obtuse, or right.

13. ∠BOC —————— -

14. ∠BOF —————— -

15. ∠AOD ———— ————

16. ∠FOG ——————————

◆ Add or subtract.

17. $4\dfrac{2}{3}$
   $+\ 2\dfrac{2}{5}$

18. $8\dfrac{3}{9}$
   $+\ 3\dfrac{5}{6}$

19. $4\dfrac{1}{10}$
   $-\ 1\dfrac{5}{6}$

20. $4\dfrac{2}{9}$
   $-\ 2\dfrac{5}{8}$

21. $11\dfrac{1}{4}$
   $-\ 8\dfrac{7}{9}$

22. $5\dfrac{4}{6}$
   $+\ 4\dfrac{5}{8}$

23. $4\dfrac{4}{5}$
   $+\ 5\dfrac{5}{12}$

24. $8\dfrac{3}{15}$
   $-\ 6\dfrac{8}{9}$

Bonus Box:
How many years and months until you are eligible to vote?

◆ Divide. Always simplify when possible.

1. $\dfrac{4}{5} \div \dfrac{2}{10} =$

2. $\dfrac{4}{7} \div \dfrac{8}{14} =$

3. $9 \div \dfrac{3}{5} =$

4. $12 \div \dfrac{6}{7} =$

5. $\dfrac{8}{15} \div \dfrac{4}{6} =$

6. $\dfrac{9}{12} \div \dfrac{3}{4} =$

7. $12 \div \dfrac{3}{4} =$

8. $\dfrac{9}{14} \div \dfrac{3}{7} =$

9. $\dfrac{2}{3} \div \dfrac{4}{6} =$

10. $\dfrac{4}{18} \div \dfrac{2}{6} =$

11. $\dfrac{5}{16} \div \dfrac{10}{20} =$

12. $10 \div \dfrac{5}{6} =$

◆ Draw and shade in shapes that have the specified area.

13. 13 sq. units

14. 11 sq. units

15. $\dfrac{1}{2}$ sq. units

◆ Multiply.

16. $\dfrac{2}{3} \times \dfrac{3}{4} =$

17. $\dfrac{2}{5} \times \dfrac{6}{7} =$

18. $\dfrac{2}{12} \times \dfrac{3}{4} =$

19. $\dfrac{2}{5} \times \dfrac{5}{6} =$

20. $\dfrac{2}{11} \times \dfrac{3}{4} =$

21. $\dfrac{2}{15} \times \dfrac{3}{8} =$

22. $\dfrac{11}{12} \times \dfrac{4}{5} =$

23. $\dfrac{2}{9} \times \dfrac{6}{7} =$

24. $\dfrac{4}{5} \times \dfrac{10}{12} =$

Bonus Box:
How long until you can apply for a driver's license? Write your answer in months. weeks, and days.

Name _____

◆ Divide. Always simplify when possible.

1. $4\frac{2}{3} \div 2\frac{1}{3} =$

2. $3\frac{1}{2} \div 2\frac{4}{5} =$

3. $3\frac{2}{9} \div 4\frac{1}{5} =$

4. $5\frac{6}{7} \div 2\frac{3}{8} =$

5. $7\frac{1}{4} \div 3\frac{1}{6} =$

6. $6\frac{2}{8} \div \times 3\frac{4}{5} =$

7. $4\frac{2}{12} \div 3\frac{2}{8} =$

8. $3\frac{3}{15} \div 4\frac{2}{3} =$

9. $7\frac{2}{14} \div 4\frac{3}{7} =$

10. $2\frac{8}{9} \div 3\frac{1}{4} =$

11. $8\frac{1}{18} \div 3\frac{2}{9} =$

12. $10\frac{3}{18} \div 3\frac{2}{9} =$

◆ Make a tree diagram to factor these numbers to their primes.

13. 100

14. 144

15. 250

◆ Add or subtract.

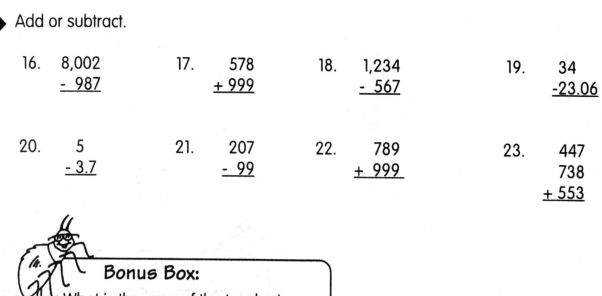

16.   8,002
     − 987

17.   578
     + 999

18.   1,234
     − 567

19.   34
     −23.06

20.   5
     − 3.7

21.   207
     − 99

22.   789
     + 999

23.   447
       738
     + 553

Bonus Box:
What is the area of the teacher's desk? Write your answer in square inches.

Name _____

◆ Divide. Always simplify when possible.

1. $2\frac{3}{7} \div 2\frac{3}{8} =$

2. $6\frac{8}{9} \div 3\frac{2}{3} =$

3. $2\frac{3}{15} \div 2\frac{1}{6} =$

4. $8\frac{4}{5} \div 2\frac{1}{5} =$

5. $5\frac{1}{2} \div 2\frac{1}{3} =$

6. $8\frac{5}{10} \div 4\frac{1}{5} =$

7. $8\frac{1}{18} \div 3\frac{1}{4} =$

8. $10\frac{2}{3} \div 5\frac{1}{6} =$

9. $12\frac{2}{6} \div 6\frac{1}{4} =$

10. $8\frac{2}{5} \div 2\frac{1}{7} =$

11. $5\frac{1}{7} \div 3\frac{1}{2} =$

12. $3\frac{2}{8} \div 2\frac{2}{3} =$

◆ Write the equivalent measurements.

13. 32 kg = _____ g

14. 4L = _____ mL

15. 30,000L = _____ kL

16. 78 mm = _____ cm

17. 1,440m = _____ km

18. 400 g = _____ kg

19. 418 g = _____ kg

20. 8,000 mL = _____ L

21. 4 L = ——— mL

◆ Multiply.

22.   593
      x 54

23.   409
      x 99

24.   63.7
      x 8.7

25.   4.125
      x 4.09

26.   999
      x 678

27. 44.238
      x 1.3

28.   54.8
      x .08

29.   8.56
      x .34

Bonus Box:
Ask ten people their favorite color. Make a graph displaying this information.

Name _____

◆ Divide. Always simplify when possible.

1. $\dfrac{1}{3} \div \dfrac{4}{6} =$

2. $4\dfrac{1}{2} \div 6 =$

3. $8 \div \dfrac{4}{5} =$

4. $\dfrac{9}{10} \div \dfrac{3}{5} =$

5. $\dfrac{4}{5} \div \dfrac{4}{5} =$

6. $12\dfrac{2}{3} \div 3\dfrac{3}{4} =$

7. $\dfrac{4}{12} \div \dfrac{2}{3} =$

8. $2\dfrac{1}{2} \div 2\dfrac{1}{4} =$

9. $25\dfrac{4}{5} \div 5\dfrac{1}{4} =$

10. $\dfrac{8}{11} \div \dfrac{2}{3} =$

11. $8\dfrac{1}{4} \div 2\dfrac{1}{6} =$

12. $4\dfrac{3}{16} \div 2\dfrac{4}{5} =$

◆ Remember the order of operations.

13. $(4 \times 5) - (6 \times 2) + 2 =$

14. $6 \times 7 + (5 - 3) \div 2 =$

15. $19 + (18 \div 3) + 10 \div 2 =$

16. $(3 \times 8) \times (8 - 6) \div 2 =$

17. $15 - 3 + 8 \times 2 \div 4 =$

18. $37 - (6 \times 3) + 5 \div 2 =$

◆ Use this number to answer the following questions. 123,456,789.987654

What number is in the:

19. tenths place? _____
20. ten thousandths place? _____
21. millionths place? _____
22. hundredths place? _____
23. thousands place? _____

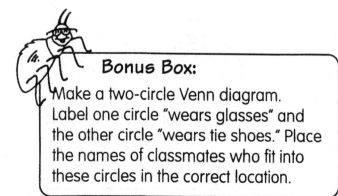

Bonus Box:
Make a two-circle Venn diagram.
Label one circle "wears glasses" and
the other circle "wears tie shoes." Place
the names of classmates who fit into
these circles in the correct location.

Name _____

◆ Divide. Always simplify when possible.

1. $5 \div \frac{3}{7} =$

2. $\frac{5}{6} \div \frac{5}{6} =$

3. $\frac{9}{10} \div \frac{4}{5} =$

4. $16 \div \frac{4}{5} =$

5. $3\frac{1}{2} \div 2\frac{1}{3} =$

6. $18\frac{2}{3} \div 6\frac{3}{8} =$

7. $4\frac{2}{5} \div 2\frac{3}{8} =$

8. $15\frac{4}{5} \div 3\frac{1}{2} =$

9. $\frac{3}{18} \div \frac{4}{15} =$

10. $\frac{8}{9} \div \frac{2}{3} =$

11. $16\frac{3}{4} \div 4\frac{1}{2} =$

12. $8 \div \frac{6}{7} =$

◆ Solve the following coin problems.

13. What coins add to 79¢ if you have no half dollars? _____

14. What coins add to 38¢ if you have no quarters? _____

15. What coins add to 93¢ if you have no dimes? _____

16. What coins add to 45¢ if you have no dimes? _____

◆ Multiply.

17.
```
  436
x  27
```

18.
```
 6.09
x .78
```

19.
```
16.54
x 6.07
```

20.
```
4,362
x 563
```

21.
```
56.003
x    .07
```

22.
```
  54
x 34
```

23.
```
 278
x 670
```

24.
```
 89.3
x 5.4
```

Bonus Box:
Make a bar graph with the letters of the alphabet on the horizontal line and a number line on the vertical. Graph the number of students whose first name begins with each letter.

◆ Write the decimals as percents and the percents as decimals.

1. 93%	2. 0.70	3. 75%	4. 0.5
5. 0.34	6. 63%	7. 9	8. 12.5%
9. 450%	10. 73.5%	11. 0.54	12. 1.5

◆ Round:

13. 345.784 to the tenths place _____

14. 5,873.8932 to the hundredths place _____

15. 544.89898 to the ten thousandths place _____

16. 7,809.9035 to the thousandths place _____

17. 55,482,449.3389878 to the millionths place _____

◆ Multiply.

18. $3\frac{2}{5} \times 7\frac{6}{8} =$

19. $15\frac{2}{3} \times 2\frac{1}{5} =$

20. $4\frac{2}{5} \times 3\frac{2}{4} =$

21. $3\frac{2}{4} \times 2\frac{1}{2} =$

22. $8\frac{4}{7} \times 3\frac{2}{9} =$

23. $9\frac{4}{5} \times 3\frac{6}{7} =$

Bonus Box:
Make a bar graph showing the distribution of the birthdays of yourself and ten friends over a 12-month period.

Name _____

◆ Write each percent as a fraction or mixed number in simplest form and each fraction as a percent.

1. 96%

2. 175%

3. $\frac{1}{2}$

4. $33\frac{1}{3}\%$

5. $\frac{3}{8}$

6. $\frac{8}{100}$

7. 110%

8. $\frac{2}{5}$

9. $2\frac{1}{2}\%$

10. $1\frac{3}{100}$

11. $\frac{5}{8}$

12. 275%

◆ Find the area. Each square = I square unit.

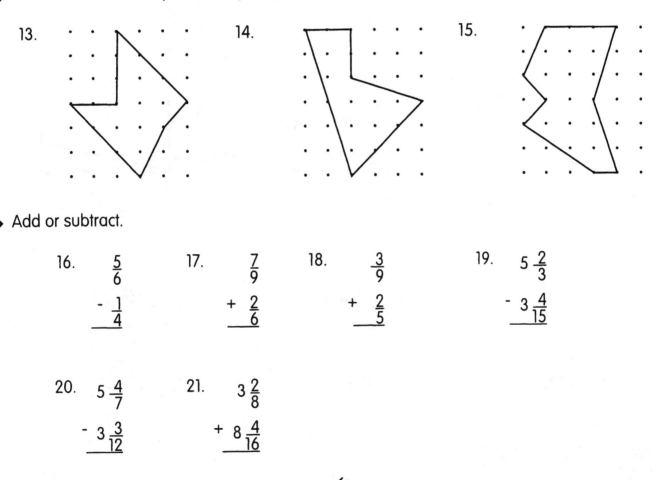

13.

14.

15.

◆ Add or subtract.

16. $\frac{5}{6}$
$-\frac{1}{4}$

17. $\frac{7}{9}$
$+\frac{2}{6}$

18. $\frac{3}{9}$
$+\frac{2}{5}$

19. $5\frac{2}{3}$
$-3\frac{4}{15}$

20. $5\frac{4}{7}$
$-3\frac{3}{12}$

21. $3\frac{2}{8}$
$+8\frac{4}{16}$

22. $5\frac{5}{8}$
$+8\frac{3}{18}$

23. $8\frac{5}{16}$
$-3\frac{7}{10}$

Bonus Box:
Draw a figure with at least two parallel lines, one right angle, and straight sides.

Name _____

◆ Figure the percent.

1. What percent of 20 is 15? _____
2. 16 is what percent of 32? _____

3. 30 is what percent of 20? _____
4. What percent of 500 is 1? _____

5. What percent of 240 is 60? _____
6. 80 is what percent of 1,600? _____

7. What percent of 100 is 30? _____
8. 40 is what percent of 200? _____

9. What percent of 18 is 6? _____
10. 200 is what percent of 100? _____

◆ You may use an angle only once as you name angles that are:

11. acute _____
12. obtuse _____
13. right _____
14. acute _____
15. obtuse _____

◆ Divide.

16. $6\overline{)674}$

17. $.9\overline{)8953}$

18. $3.2\overline{)6.004}$

19. $.008\overline{)68.908}$

20. $5\overline{)7823}$

21. $.98\overline{)1065}$

Bonus Box:
Draw a figure with at least one set of parallel lines, two acute angles, and two obtuse angles.

◆ Figure the percent.

1. 25 is what percent of 50? _____

2. What percent of 500 is 50? _____

3. 300 is what percent of 200? _____

4. 13 is what percent of 104? _____

5. What percent of 100 is 25? _____

6. What percent of 150 is 37.5? _____

7. 60 is what percent of 240? _____

8. 20 is what percent of 200? _____

9. What percent of 300 is 45? _____

10. 30 is what percent of 150? _____

◆ What is the largest common factor of each group of numbers?

11. 4, 8, 12

12. 21, 42, 56

13. 20, 40, 80

14. 60, 30, 45

15. 19, 57, 38

16. 15, 30, 35

17. 24, 32, 40

18. 27, 81, 63

19. 64, 72, 56

◆ Add or subtract.

20.
```
   5.06
 -2.135
```

21.
```
 89,345
-23,768
```

22.
```
  689
 +592
```

23.
```
    89
    78
    37
    25
    94
 +  61
```

24.
```
 8,003
 - 675
```

25.
```
  5,689
    438
+ 1,842
```

26.
```
    4
 - 1.3
```

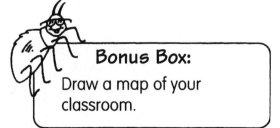

Bonus Box:
Draw a map of your classroom.

◆ Find the number.

1. 50% of what number is 34? _____
2. 5% of what number is 6? _____
3. 18 is 90% of what number? _____
4. 12 is 5% of what number? _____
5. 75% of what number is 45? _____
6. 400 is 125% of what number? _____
7. 3 is 2½% of what number? _____
8. 30 is 60% of what number? _____
9. 66⅔% of what number is 12? _____
10. 120 is 60% of what number? _____

◆ Convert these times.

11. 45 minutes = _____ hour
12. 15 minutes = _____ seconds

13. 12 hours = _____ day
14. 36 hours = _____ days

15. 21 days = _____ weeks
16. 2 days = _____ hours

◆ Round to the correct place.

17. Round 512,246,972 to the millions place _____

18. Round 358,937,275 to the thousands place _____

19. Round 345,829,015 to the ten thousands place _____

20. Round 539,257,316 to the hundred thousands place _____

21. Round 435,916,367 to the ten millions place _____

22. Round 361,793,263 to the hundred millions place _____

Bonus Box:

Make a daily time schedule for yourself. Include sleeping, eating, school, homework, and all the other normal daily activities you have.

◆ Find the number that equals X in each statement.

1. 35 is 12.5% of X. _____

2. 45% of X is 9. _____

3. 40% of X is 82. _____

4. 0.5% of X is 6. _____

5. 92% of X is 368. _____

6. 10.5 is 14% of X. _____

7. 18 is 20% of X. _____

8. 52 is 130% of X. _____

9. 65% of X is 104. _____

10. 12 is 15% of X. _____

◆ Remember the order of operations.

11. (5 x 60) + (7 x 3) - 7 =

12. 84 ÷ 2 x (14 x 2) =

13. 9 x (5 + 3) ÷ 2 =

14. 8 + 7 - 6 x 5 ÷ 4 =

15. 6 x 7 x 5 + 10 ÷ 5 =

16. 11 x (2 x 2) ÷ 4 =

17. 10 + 15 ÷ (9 ÷ 3) =

18. 35 ÷ 5 + (42 ÷ 7) + 3 =

◆ Find the average.

19. 45, 46, 45, 44, 47, 46

20. 100, 75, 85, 75, 34

21. 23, 25, 24, 26, 27, 25

22. 83, 85, 92, 84, 45, 95, 81

23. 4.5, 6.5, 7.5, 6, 5, 7

24. 75, 77, 76, 0, 79, 74, 77

25. 85, 86, 89, 85, 0, 87, 88

26. 69, 68, 69, 68, 66, 95

Bonus Box:
How many hours will you spend in this class in one semester? Show your answer and your work.

◆ Find the percents.

1. 56% of 300 _____
2. 14% of 50 _____
3. 10% of 60 _____
4. 20% of 39 _____
5. 30% of 18 _____
6. 15% of 50 _____
7. 70% of 80 _____
8. 10% of 15 _____
9. 50% of 18 _____
10. 90% of 130 _____
11. 40% of 65 _____
12. 80% of 120 _____

◆ Convert the following measurements.

13. 2,200 yards = ——— miles

14. 2 miles = _____ yards

15. ⅝ mile = ——————— feet

16. 42 inches = _____ feet

17. ½ mile = ——————— feet

18. 7 yards = _____ feet

19. 5 feet = ——————— inches

20. 6 yards, 60 inches = _____ feet

21. 8 ⅓ yards = ——— feet

22. 84 inches = _____ feet

◆ Add or subtract.

23. $4\frac{2}{7}$
   $-2\frac{2}{3}$

24. $\frac{5}{16}$
   $+\frac{15}{16}$

25. $7\frac{1}{3}$
   $-2\frac{5}{6}$

26. $9\frac{1}{5}$
   $-4\frac{6}{7}$

27. $4\frac{8}{10}$
   $+5\frac{4}{5}$

28. $\frac{7}{9}$
   $+\frac{5}{6}$

29. $6\frac{3}{8}$
   $-5\frac{3}{4}$

30. $\frac{5}{6}$
   $+\frac{4}{5}$

List three ways you use math when you go shopping.

◆ Figure the percent.

1. Find 85% of 80. _____

2. 32 is what percent of 96? _____

3. What percent of 75 is 15? _____

4. Find 35% of 160. _____

5. Find 18% of 1,200. _____

6. Find 150% of 50. _____

7. 22 is what percent of 50? _____

8. What percent of 40 is 100? _____

9. 45% of what number is 9? _____

10. 510 is 85% of what number? _____

◆ Extend each pattern three steps.

11. 1, 2, 5, 10, 13, 26, 29, _____, _____, _____

12. 1, 3, 5, 15, 17, 51, 53, _____, _____, _____

13. 1, 4, 16, 64, 256, 1,024, _____, _____, _____

14. 1, 2, 4, 5, 7, 8, 10, 11, _____, _____, _____

◆ Divide.

15. $1.2\overline{)89.5}$

16. $42\overline{)5067}$

17. $6.03\overline{)678}$

18. $.08\overline{)1.058}$

19. $59\overline{)7809}$

20. $3.5\overline{)87.25}$

Bonus Box:
Write a story problem for a classmate to solve. The answer must be a fraction.

Name _____

◆ Figure the percent.

1. What percent of 500 is 75?

2. 15 is what percent of 120?

3. 85% of what number is 102?

4. Find 90% of 20.

5. 3.75 is 1% of what number?

6. 1.8 is 2.4% of what number?

7. Find 15% of 20.

8. What percent of 27 is 18?

9. Find 125% of 80.

10. Find 20% of 300.

◆ Write the equivalent measurement.

11. 4 gal 3 qt. = _____ qt.

12. 7 gal = _____ qt.

13. 72 fl oz. = _____ qt.

14. 2 qt. = _____ fl. oz.

15. 7 pt = _____ c

16. 4 pt = _____ fl. oz.

17. 6 lb = _____ oz.

18. 12 fl oz. = _____ c

◆ Multiply.

19. 178
    x 56

20. 6509
    x 428

21. 56.238
    x 3.45

22. 836
    x 34

23. 7.421
    x .45

24. 295
    x 33

25. 591.2
    x .64

26. 608
    x 52

Bonus Box:
List five businesses in your community whose employees need math.

Name _____

◆ Write yes or no under each ratio to tell whether or not it is equal.

1. $\frac{6}{16} = \frac{9}{24}$

2. $\frac{12}{18} = \frac{8}{9}$

3. $\frac{24}{27} = \frac{48}{63}$

4. $\frac{9}{6} = \frac{15}{10}$

5. $\frac{2}{5} = \frac{5}{9}$

6. $\frac{3}{12} = \frac{25}{100}$

7. $\frac{30}{40} = \frac{80}{100}$

8. $\frac{15}{10} = \frac{9}{8}$

9. $\frac{21}{9} = \frac{7}{3}$

10. $\frac{2}{4} = \frac{5}{9}$

11. $\frac{40}{50} = \frac{50}{40}$

12. $\frac{8}{4} = \frac{210}{105}$

◆ Draw and shade in shapes that have the specified area.

13. 11 sq. units

14. 14 sq. units

15. $13\frac{1}{2}$ sq. units

◆ What is the smallest common multiple for each group of numbers?

16. 3, 6, 2

17. 7, 8, 2

18. 5, 15, 3

19. 10, 15, 5

20. 9, 6, 3

21. 4, 6, 8

22. 3, 4, 5

23. 5, 6, 2

24. 3, 8, 6

Bonus Box:
Ask at least five friends whether they like vanilla, chocolate, or strawberry ice cream best. Then make a graph showing the results of your survey.

Name _____

◆ Solve each proportion.

1. $\dfrac{8}{12} = \dfrac{6}{x}$

2. $\dfrac{3}{9} = \dfrac{x}{15}$

3. $\dfrac{12}{x} = \dfrac{8}{10}$

4. $\dfrac{15}{9} = \dfrac{x}{33}$

5. $\dfrac{9}{x} = \dfrac{30}{40}$

6. $\dfrac{7}{8} = \dfrac{14}{x}$

7. $\dfrac{x}{18} = \dfrac{4}{6}$

8. $\dfrac{6}{15} = \dfrac{x}{25}$

9. $\dfrac{6}{10} = \dfrac{60}{x}$

10. $\dfrac{9}{3} = \dfrac{12}{x}$

11. $\dfrac{x}{12} = \dfrac{12}{18}$

12. $\dfrac{3}{x} = \dfrac{10}{30}$

◆ Write the missing number.

13. 88 mm = _____ cm

14. 1,314 g = _____ kg

15. 1550 m = _____ km

16. 6,076 mg = _____ g

17. 13 m = _____ cm

18. 12 g = _____ mg

19. 2,356 m = _____ km

20. 365 m = _____ km

◆ Multiply.

21. $8\dfrac{3}{5} \times 2\dfrac{1}{4} =$

22. $3\dfrac{1}{4} \times 3\dfrac{1}{3} =$

23. $\dfrac{6}{7} \times \dfrac{2}{3} =$

24. $2\dfrac{7}{8} \times 3\dfrac{2}{5} =$

25. $\dfrac{4}{5} \times \dfrac{3}{4} =$

26. $5\dfrac{4}{7} \times 3 =$

27. $7\dfrac{2}{9} \times 2\dfrac{2}{6} =$

28. $9\dfrac{3}{8} \times 3\dfrac{2}{4} =$

29. $\dfrac{5}{6} \times \dfrac{3}{4} =$

Bonus Box:
What is the volume of your school locker? Show your answer and your work.

◆ Solve each proportion.

1. $\dfrac{6}{8} = \dfrac{9}{x}$

2. $\dfrac{x}{3.6} = \dfrac{75}{100}$

3. $\dfrac{x}{4} = \dfrac{90}{15}$

4. $\dfrac{33}{x} = \dfrac{6}{2}$

5. $\dfrac{x}{5} = \dfrac{94}{1}$

6. $\dfrac{4}{28} = \dfrac{x}{42}$

7. $\dfrac{4}{x} = \dfrac{16}{20}$

8. $\dfrac{5}{10} = \dfrac{x}{25}$

9. $\dfrac{x}{7} = \dfrac{9}{21}$

10. $\dfrac{15}{45} = \dfrac{14}{x}$

11. $\dfrac{x}{90} = \dfrac{15}{60}$

12. $\dfrac{3.5}{10.5} = \dfrac{5}{x}$

◆ Solve. Remember the order of operations.

13. $5 \times (6 \times 3) + 5 - 6 \div 2 =$

14. $25 \div 5 \times (3 \times 6) \div 3 =$

15. $(7 \times 7 - 1) \div 6 \div 2 + 6 =$

16. $6 \div 2 \times (25 \div 5) + 3 =$

17. $29 + (16 \div 4) \div 2 =$

18. $9 \times 4 \div 2 + 7 - 5 =$

◆ Divide.

19. $\dfrac{7}{8} \div \dfrac{2}{3}$

20. $2\dfrac{6}{7} \div 2\dfrac{1}{4} =$

21. $\dfrac{5}{6} \div \dfrac{3}{5} =$

22. $4\dfrac{3}{7} \div 3 =$

23. $5\dfrac{2}{4} \div 2\dfrac{6}{7} =$

24. $\dfrac{5}{3} \div \dfrac{9}{10} =$

25. $8 \div 2\dfrac{1}{4} =$

26. $6\dfrac{3}{5} \div \dfrac{15}{16} =$

27. $\dfrac{5}{8} \div \dfrac{7}{10} =$

Bonus Box:
Write both a fraction and a decimal to show how many of the people in your class are left-handed.

◆ Find the rate:

1. per hour if you drive 220 miles in 4 hours. _____
2. per minute if your heart beats 234 times in 3 minutes. _____
3. per can if you pay $1.68 for 6 cans of pop. _____
4. per hour if it snows 3 inches in 4 hours. _____
5. per minute if you type 240 words in 5 minutes. _____
6. per ounce if you spend $3.49 for a 20-ounce box of cereal. _____
7. per pound if you spend $1.30 for a 5-pound bag of potatoes. _____
8. per day if you consume 13,300 calories in 7 days. _____
9. per gallon if you pay $2.25 for a 0.5-gallon container of frozen yogurt. _____
10. per gallon if you pay $10.80 for 8 gallons of cider. _____

◆ Write the fraction as a percent and as a decimal.

11. $\dfrac{1}{8}$

12. $\dfrac{5}{10}$

13. $\dfrac{8}{10}$

14. $\dfrac{3}{8}$

15. $\dfrac{3}{4}$

16. $\dfrac{1}{4}$

17. $\dfrac{90}{100}$

18. $\dfrac{10}{100}$

19. $\dfrac{40}{50}$

◆ Subtract.

20. $\dfrac{6}{7} - \dfrac{1}{3} =$

21. $5\dfrac{2}{3} - \dfrac{2}{9} =$

22. $\dfrac{16}{20} - \dfrac{2}{5} =$

23. $\dfrac{9}{10} - \dfrac{1}{2} =$

24. $\dfrac{7}{8} - \dfrac{4}{6} =$

25. $2\dfrac{1}{5} - \dfrac{7}{10} =$

26. $8\dfrac{1}{4} - \dfrac{7}{8} =$

27. $3 - \dfrac{6}{15} =$

28. $7\dfrac{1}{5} - 3\dfrac{14}{15} =$

Bonus Box:
Using the numbers from your locker, rearrange them to make the smallest number you can.

Name _____

◆ You have a number cube with the numbers 1, 2, 3, 4, 5, and 6 on the faces. If you roll it once, what is the probability of getting:

1. the number 3? _____

2. a number other than 4? _____

3. an odd number? _____

4. a number smaller than 6? _____

5. the number 2? _____

6. a number greater than 2? _____

7. an even number? _____

8. a number greater than 1? _____

9. the numbers 4 or 5? _____

10. the numbers 1, 2, or 3? _____

◆ Find the area.

11.

15 mm

20 mm

12.

8 mm

18 mm

13.

18 mm

12 mm

◆ Add or subtract.

14. $\begin{array}{r} 4 \\ -0.58 \\ \hline \end{array}$

15. $\begin{array}{r} 704 \\ -65.53 \\ \hline \end{array}$

16. $\begin{array}{r} 435.008 \\ -59.84 \\ \hline \end{array}$

17. $\begin{array}{r} 7.382 \\ -2.4963 \\ \hline \end{array}$

18. $\begin{array}{r} 556.748 \\ +427.812 \\ \hline \end{array}$

19. $\begin{array}{r} 11.89 \\ +4.006 \\ \hline \end{array}$

20. $\begin{array}{r} 339.7 \\ +1.067 \\ \hline \end{array}$

21. $\begin{array}{r} 932.7 \\ +85.09 \\ \hline \end{array}$

Bonus Box:
Ask at least eight people whether they like football, basketball, or baseball best. Then construct a circle graph to display the results of your survey.

Name _____

◆ You have a sack with two yellow marbles, three green marbles, one blue marble, and two red marbles. With one draw, what is the probability of getting:

1. a blue marble? _____

2. a red or blue marble? _____

3. a yellow marble? _____

4. a blue or green marble? _____

5. a red marble? _____

6. a red or green marble? _____

7. a green marble? _____

8. a blue or yellow marble? _____

9. any marble but blue? _____

10. any marble but yellow? _____

◆ Find the measure of the missing angle in each triangle.

11.

80°
40°

12.

100° 30°

13.

45°

90°

◆ Multiply.

14. $\frac{6}{8} \times \frac{4}{7} =$

15. $3\frac{1}{2} \times 2\frac{3}{4} =$

16. $\frac{3}{5} \times \frac{10}{12} =$

17. $\frac{3}{8} \times \frac{4}{5} =$

18. $\frac{11}{12} \times \frac{3}{8} =$

19. $\frac{2}{3} \times \frac{3}{10} =$

20. $5\frac{2}{5} \times 3\frac{2}{3} =$

21. $\frac{1}{9} \times \frac{5}{6} =$

22. $2\frac{2}{5} \times 3\frac{3}{9} =$

Bonus Box:
List five examples of parallel lines in your classroom.

Name _____

◆ Home runs in a season: 38, 42, 36, 17, 38, 21, 24, 38

Find: 1. the range _____   2. the median _____

         3. the mode _____   4. the mean _____

Points scored: 19, 17, 18, 19, 16, 6, 10, 12, 9

Find: 5. the range _____   6. the median _____

         7. the mode _____   8. the mean _____

◆ Write each fraction as a decimal.

9. $\dfrac{3}{4}$ 10. $\dfrac{6}{8}$ 11. $\dfrac{1}{4}$ 12. $\dfrac{9}{10}$

13. $\dfrac{1}{8}$ 14. $\dfrac{8}{10}$ 15. $\dfrac{4}{5}$ 16. $\dfrac{1}{5}$

◆ Find x.

17. $\dfrac{4}{5} = \dfrac{x}{10}$ 18. $\dfrac{x}{8} = \dfrac{12}{20}$ 19. $\dfrac{5}{8} = \dfrac{15}{x}$

20. $\dfrac{2}{5} = \dfrac{6}{x}$ 21. $\dfrac{4}{6} = \dfrac{6}{x}$ 22. $\dfrac{4}{9} = \dfrac{5}{x}$

Bonus Box:
Make a time line with at least five events in your life appropriately marked and identified.

Name _____

◆ Points scored: 25, 23, 12, 17, 16, 10, 16, 8, 16

Find: 1.   the range _____   2.   the median _____

          3.   the mode _____   4.   the mean _____

Tickets sold: 45, 63, 46, 72, 63, 38, 41, 56, 55

Find: 5.   the range _____   6.   the median _____

          7.   the mode _____   8.   the mean _____

◆ Find the circumference. Use 3.14 for π.

9.   10.   11.

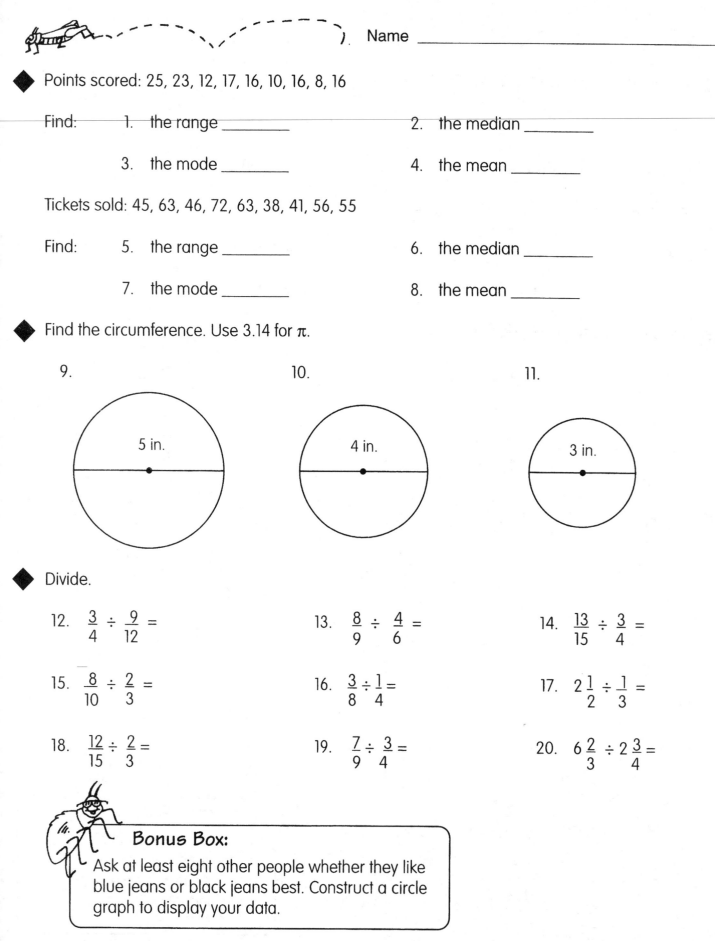

5 in.   4 in.   3 in.

◆ Divide.

12. $\dfrac{3}{4} \div \dfrac{9}{12} =$ 13. $\dfrac{8}{9} \div \dfrac{4}{6} =$ 14. $\dfrac{13}{15} \div \dfrac{3}{4} =$

15. $\dfrac{8}{10} \div \dfrac{2}{3} =$ 16. $\dfrac{3}{8} \div \dfrac{1}{4} =$ 17. $2\dfrac{1}{2} \div \dfrac{1}{3} =$

18. $\dfrac{12}{15} \div \dfrac{2}{3} =$ 19. $\dfrac{7}{9} \div \dfrac{3}{4} =$ 20. $6\dfrac{2}{3} \div 2\dfrac{3}{4} =$

Bonus Box:
Ask at least eight other people whether they like blue jeans or black jeans best. Construct a circle graph to display your data.

Name _____

◆ Determine the variable.

1. $m + 15 = 35$ 2. $64 + x = 82$ 3. $y + 75 = 84$

4. $n + 33 = 56$ 5. $32 + w = 48$ 6. $15 + z = 78$

7. $34 + m = 65$ 8. $n + 15 = 37$ 9. $x + 52 = 97$

10. $48 + z = 71$ 11. $43 + k = 55$ 12. $s + 53 = 78$

◆ Find the area.

13.   14.   15.

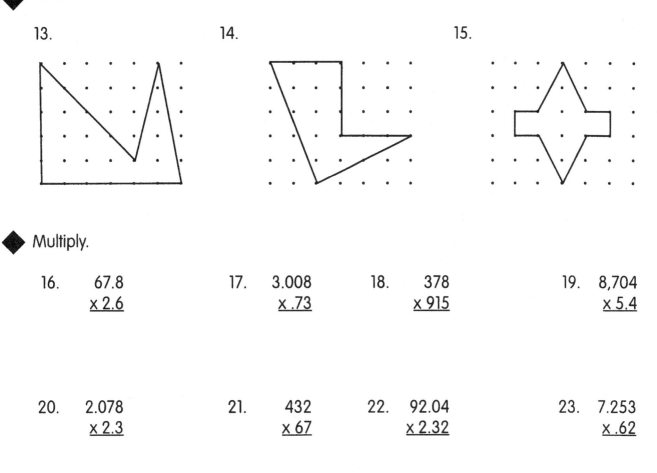

◆ Multiply.

16.   67.8   17.   3.008   18.   378   19.   8,704
      x 2.6   x .73   x 915   x 5.4

20.   2.078   21.   432   22.   92.04   23.   7.253
      x 2.3   x 67   x 2.32   x .62

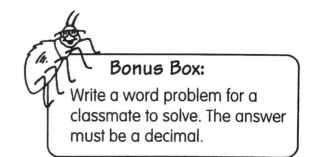

Bonus Box:
Write a word problem for a classmate to solve. The answer must be a decimal.

◆ Determine the variable.

1. $x + 2.5 = 11$ 2. $4 + x = 7.2$ 3. $17 + z = 52$

4. $a + 4.5 = 16$ 5. $z + 13.3 = 23.5$ 6. $25 + b = 67$

7. $b + 28.9 = 63$ 8. $14 + n = 55.5$ 9. $x + 25.5 = 53$

10. $12.2 + z = 19$ 11. $n + 21.6 = 25$ 12. $x + 45 = 60$

◆ Write each decimal as a fraction.

13. .25   14. .125   15. .375

16. .75   17. .6   18. .625

19. .2   20. .8   21. .875

◆ Add or subtract.

22. $\dfrac{4}{5}$ 23. $\dfrac{8}{9}$ 24. $\dfrac{2}{8}$ 25. $2\dfrac{1}{9}$
    $-\dfrac{2}{7}$ $-\dfrac{3}{10}$ $+\dfrac{3}{5}$ $-\dfrac{5}{6}$

26. $\dfrac{4}{7}$ 27. $5\dfrac{2}{9}$ 28. $\dfrac{4}{7}$ 29. $4\dfrac{5}{8}$
    $+\dfrac{2}{3}$ $-3\dfrac{4}{5}$ $+\dfrac{8}{9}$ $+\dfrac{7}{8}$

Bonus Box:
Find an example of a tessellation in your school.

◆ Determine the variable.

1. $n - 4.2 = 5$ 2. $13.9 - x = 4$ 3. $76 - z = 32$

4. $m - 33 = 152$ 5. $z - 28 = 57$ 6. $m - 41 = 65$

7. $y - 15 = 75$ 8. $c - 25 = 38$ 9. $m - 6 = 19$

10. $43 - a = 34$ 11. $67 - x = 24$ 12. $71 - x = 4.3$

◆ Find the mean.

13. 56, 45, 57, 47, 58, 52, 45   14. 29, 28, 27, 28, 29, 27, 26, 25

15. 5, 7, 6, 8, 4, 5, 3, 6, 5, 4   16. 99, 98, 97, 95, 98, 97, 0, 96

17. 88, 87, 89, 86, 88, 87, 85   18. 56, 57, 54, 55, 56, 53, 0, 55

◆ Find x.

19. $\dfrac{3}{5} = \dfrac{10}{x}$ 20. $\dfrac{x}{8} = \dfrac{2}{4}$ 21. $\dfrac{9}{10} = \dfrac{6}{x}$

22. $\dfrac{64}{16} = \dfrac{x}{15}$ 23. $\dfrac{1.5}{6} = \dfrac{2}{x}$ 24. $\dfrac{3}{8} = \dfrac{x}{10}$

25. $\dfrac{36}{81} = \dfrac{9}{x}$ 26. $\dfrac{x}{5} = \dfrac{7}{10}$ 27. $\dfrac{42}{x} = \dfrac{8}{6}$

Bonus Box:

Make a Venn diagram with three circles overlapping each other. Label one circle "wears earring(s)," the second circle "wears glasses," and the third circle "wears athletic shoes." Put the names of your classmates where they appropriately fit in the circles.

◆ Determine the variable.

1. r - 3.5 = 16   2. c - 11 = 7   3. t - 40.8 = 36.2

4. r - 10.5 = 94   5. 65 - z = 43.8   6. 87 - b = 22.2

7. d - 34.5 = 23.4   8. 11 - z = .11   9. 46 - t = 32.9

10. 53 - x = 3.5   11. t - 8.9 = 15   12. 503 - t = 305

◆ Find the area. Use 3.14 for π.

13.   14.   15.

5 in.   7 in.   3 in.

◆ Divide.

16. .9〉45.8   17. 45〉8,734   18. .054〉784

19. 25〉756   20. .008〉6,732   21. 19〉46.3

22. 101〉873   23. 6.7〉1,045   24. .6〉7,856

Bonus Box:
Ask at least ten people whether they like dogs or cats best. Then make a pictograph to display your data.

Name _____

◆ Determine the variable.

1. $8x = 24$ 2. $4z = 18$ 3. $6c = 30$

4. $15b = 32$ 5. $8.2r = 24.6$ 6. $3z = 18$

7. $4.5z = 36$ 8. $3.8b = 22.8$ 9. $19x = 47.5$

10. $5w = 44$ 11. $7k = 63$ 12. $4.2n = 25.2$

◆ Draw and shade in a figure with the area requested.

13. 14½ sq. units   14. 9.5 sq. units   15. 11 sq. units

```
· · · · · · · ·        · · · · · · · ·        · · · · · · · ·
· · · · · · · ·        · · · · · · · ·        · · · · · · · ·
· · · · · · · ·        · · · · · · · ·        · · · · · · · ·
· · · · · · · ·        · · · · · · · ·        · · · · · · · ·
· · · · · · · ·        · · · · · · · ·        · · · · · · · ·
· · · · · · · ·        · · · · · · · ·        · · · · · · · ·
```

◆ Find x.

16. $\dfrac{8}{9} = \dfrac{9}{x}$

17. $\dfrac{x}{8} = \dfrac{10}{12}$

18. $\dfrac{4}{x} = \dfrac{8}{12}$

19. $\dfrac{36}{72} = \dfrac{7}{x}$

20. $\dfrac{x}{16} = \dfrac{3}{8}$

21. $\dfrac{20}{25} = \dfrac{7}{x}$

22. $\dfrac{7}{6} = \dfrac{9}{x}$

23. $\dfrac{9}{4} = \dfrac{10}{x}$

24. $\dfrac{12}{15} = \dfrac{18}{x}$

Bonus Box:
How much will school lunch cost you for one month?

Name _____

Determine the variable.

1. $5c = 60$

2. $8.2x = 59.04$

3. $19t = 66.5$

4. $17n = 85$

5. $17y = 42.5$

6. $9.5x = 33.25$

7. $16w = 48$

8. $8t = 28$

9. $5z = 38.5$

10. $4r = 28$

11. $15x = 18.75$

12. $9z = 67.5$

Use the circle at the right to name an example of:

13. chord

17. diameter

14. arc

18. arc

15. center

19. central angle

16. radius

20. radius

Multiply or divide.

21. $\dfrac{6}{7} \times \dfrac{3}{4} =$

22. $\dfrac{4}{5} \div \dfrac{2}{7} =$

23. $2\dfrac{1}{3} \times 6\dfrac{2}{5} =$

24. $\dfrac{15}{16} \times \dfrac{4}{8} =$

25. $\dfrac{10}{21} \times \dfrac{3}{5} =$

26. $\dfrac{4}{6} \div \dfrac{2}{3} =$

27. $\dfrac{6}{5} \div \dfrac{6}{5} =$

28. $\dfrac{18}{20} \div \dfrac{4}{5} =$

29. $\dfrac{5}{6} \times \dfrac{2}{3} =$

Bonus Box:
Draw a tessellation.

◆ Determine the variable.

1. $\dfrac{x}{6} = 7$

2. $\dfrac{z}{4} = 3$

3. $\dfrac{x}{5} = 4$

4. $\dfrac{t}{8} = 7$

5. $\dfrac{t}{3} = 5$

6. $\dfrac{r}{13} = 3$

7. $\dfrac{n}{5} = 7.5$

8. $\dfrac{v}{4} = 4$

9. $\dfrac{n}{2.5} = 7.5$

10. $\dfrac{t}{4} = 7.5$

11. $\dfrac{x}{3} = 15$

12. $\dfrac{z}{6} = 9$

◆ Write a fraction for each decimal.

13. .9

17. .6

14. .625

18. .5

15. .8

19. .25

16. .125

20. .75

◆ Add or subtract.

21.
$$\begin{array}{r} 456 \\ -222.9 \\ \hline \end{array}$$

22.
$$\begin{array}{r} 9{,}338 \\ +\ 704 \\ \hline \end{array}$$

23.
$$\begin{array}{r} 9{,}002 \\ -\ 768 \\ \hline \end{array}$$

24.
$$\begin{array}{r} 46.07 \\ -\ 23.39 \\ \hline \end{array}$$

25.
$$\begin{array}{r} 73.5 \\ +\ 18.53 \\ \hline \end{array}$$

26.
$$\begin{array}{r} 187 \\ -\ 98 \\ \hline \end{array}$$

Bonus Box:
Set up a graph with your class periods across the bottom. You are going to make a line graph showing how many students are in each of your classes throughout the day so the numbers on the left must be able to accommodate those numbers.

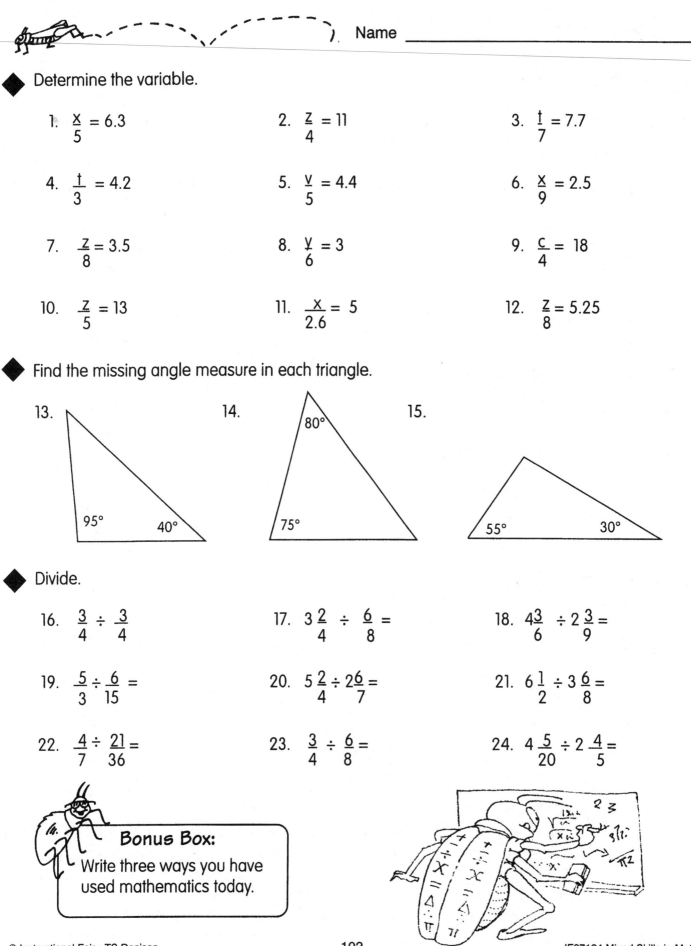

Name _____

◆ Determine the variable.

1. $\dfrac{x}{5} = 6.3$

2. $\dfrac{z}{4} = 11$

3. $\dfrac{t}{7} = 7.7$

4. $\dfrac{t}{3} = 4.2$

5. $\dfrac{v}{5} = 4.4$

6. $\dfrac{x}{9} = 2.5$

7. $\dfrac{z}{8} = 3.5$

8. $\dfrac{y}{6} = 3$

9. $\dfrac{c}{4} = 18$

10. $\dfrac{z}{5} = 13$

11. $\dfrac{x}{2.6} = 5$

12. $\dfrac{z}{8} = 5.25$

◆ Find the missing angle measure in each triangle.

13.

95°   40°

14.

80°   75°

15.

55°   30°

◆ Divide.

16. $\dfrac{3}{4} \div \dfrac{3}{4}$

17. $3\dfrac{2}{4} \div \dfrac{6}{8} =$

18. $4\dfrac{3}{6} \div 2\dfrac{3}{9} =$

19. $\dfrac{5}{3} \div \dfrac{6}{15} =$

20. $5\dfrac{2}{4} \div 2\dfrac{6}{7} =$

21. $6\dfrac{1}{2} \div 3\dfrac{6}{8} =$

22. $\dfrac{4}{7} \div \dfrac{21}{36} =$

23. $\dfrac{3}{4} \div \dfrac{6}{8} =$

24. $4\dfrac{5}{20} \div 2\dfrac{4}{5} =$

Bonus Box:
Write three ways you have
used mathematics today.

◆ Determine the variable.

1. $3x = 18$

2. $x - 43 = 17$

3. $\dfrac{x}{5} = 23$

4. $2.5x = 25$

5. $7 + z = 23$

6. $t - 5.5 = 8.5$

7. $\dfrac{t}{6} = 8$

8. $n - 14 = 27$

9. $z + 14 = 46$

10. $4n = 17$

11. $5 + y = 15$

12. $\dfrac{z}{8} = 4$

◆ Find the area.

13.

8 in.

9 in.

14.

4.5 in.

10 in.

15.

9.5 in.

9 in.

◆ Test scores: 84, 95, 96, 74, 86, 77, 79, 86, 78, 86, 81

Find the:

16. range _____

17. median _____

18. mode _____

19. mean _____

Bonus Box:
Make a list of three items served in your lunchroom which you don't like. Ask at least eight people which they dislike most. Make a bar graph of the back of this paper displaying your data.

◆ Determine the variable.

1. $4x = 72$

2. $5 + n = 37$

3. $\dfrac{t}{7} = 56$

4. $t - 34 = 48$

5. $25z = 300$

6. $r - 23 = 87$

7. $15r = 67.5$

8. $\dfrac{t}{6} = 13.8$

9. $s - 45 = 98$

10. $t + 12 = 56$

11. $34 + x = 54$

12. $\dfrac{r}{4} = 6.5$

◆ Beside each shape draw a congruent shape and a similar shape.

13.   14.   15.   16.

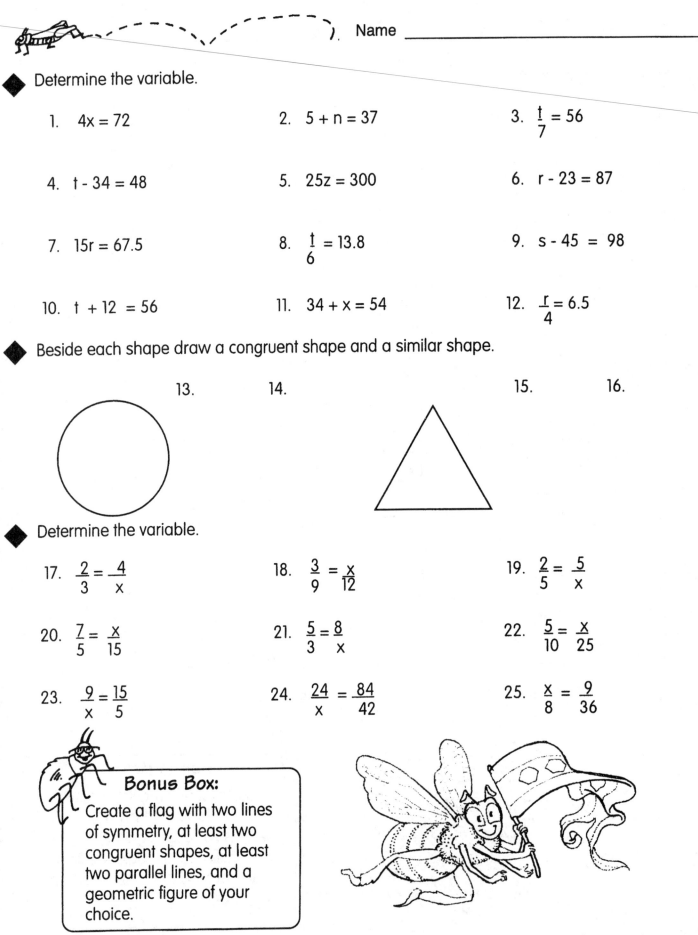

◆ Determine the variable.

17. $\dfrac{2}{3} = \dfrac{4}{x}$

18. $\dfrac{3}{9} = \dfrac{x}{12}$

19. $\dfrac{2}{5} = \dfrac{5}{x}$

20. $\dfrac{7}{5} = \dfrac{x}{15}$

21. $\dfrac{5}{3} = \dfrac{8}{x}$

22. $\dfrac{5}{10} = \dfrac{x}{25}$

23. $\dfrac{9}{x} = \dfrac{15}{5}$

24. $\dfrac{24}{x} = \dfrac{84}{42}$

25. $\dfrac{x}{8} = \dfrac{9}{36}$

Bonus Box:
Create a flag with two lines of symmetry, at least two congruent shapes, at least two parallel lines, and a geometric figure of your choice.

Name _____

◆ Write the opposite of each integer.

1. 76	2. -14	3. -6	4. 25
5. -34	6. -37	7. 14	8. 78
9. -57	10. 29	11. -15	12. 5

◆ Write a fraction for each decimal.

13. .25   14. .75

15. .3   16. .5

17. .40   18. .60

19. .08   20. .12

21. .55

◆ Determine the variable.

22. $5x = 50$

23. $\dfrac{t}{8} = 8$

24. $x - 17 = 86$

25. $z + 34 = 92$

26. $9n = 61.2$

27. $\dfrac{x}{15} = 3.2$

28. $86 - r = 15$

29. $7r = 49$

30. $3z = 28.5$

Bonus Box:
Write a word problem for a classmate to solve. The answer must be a decimal.

Name _____

◆ Find the missing integer.

1. - 7 + _____ = - 7

2. -18 • 4 = _____ • -18

3. - 9 + 1 = _____ + -9

4. _____ • 6 = 0

5. -16 • _____ = -16

6. _____ • 3 = 3

7. 8 • 0 = _____

8. _____ + 0 = 17

9. -1 • _____ = 0

10. -23 • 1 = _____

11. _____ + -1 = -1

12. -8 • _____ = - 8

◆ Find the missing angle measure.

13.

70°   47°

14.

29°   115°

15.

117°   36°

◆ Add or subtract.

16.   5.34
     + 3.759

17.   780.1
    - 256.97

18. 11,036
    - 9,558

19.   7.49
     + 9.67

20.   7
     -2.07

21.   84
     +49

22. 7,823
    -2,358

23. 2,468
    +8,675

Bonus Box:
Draw a circle graph showing the number of boys and girls in this class.

◆ Find the missing integer.

1. -25 + -75 = _____

2. -13 + -43 = _____

3. -44 + -41 = _____

4. 86 + -64 = _____

5. 46 + -89 = _____

6. -19 + -7 = _____

7. -56 + 27 = _____

8. 89 + -13 = _____

9. -19 + 75 = _____

10. -42 + -17 = _____

11. 16 + 42 = _____

12. -85 + 86 = _____

◆ Find the circumference. Use 3.14 for π.

13.

$5\frac{1}{2}$in.

14.

$4\frac{1}{2}$in.

15.

$3\frac{1}{2}$in.

◆ Multiply.

16. $\frac{2}{5} \times \frac{7}{8} =$

17. $\frac{8}{3} \times \frac{7}{4} =$

18. $2\frac{2}{3} \times 4\frac{5}{6} =$

19. $\frac{9}{8} \times \frac{5}{3} =$

20. $\frac{14}{15} \times \frac{6}{7} =$

21. $3\frac{2}{8} \times 4\frac{4}{6} =$

22. $\frac{7}{10} \times \frac{5}{9} =$

23. $\frac{18}{6} \times \frac{12}{4} =$

24. $5\frac{4}{14} \times 3\frac{6}{16} =$

Bonus Box:

Show how many different outfits you could make if you had three different pairs of jeans and three different sweatshirts.

◆ Find the missing integer.

1. -32 + -71 = _____

2. -43 + 17 = _____

3. -16 + -19 = _____

4. 25 + -37 = _____

5. -18 + -7 = _____

6. 46 + 83 = _____

7. 89 + -76 = _____

8. -43 + -15 = _____

9. -16 + 37 = _____

10. -2 + 3 = _____

11. 5 + -6 = _____

12. -27 + 13 = _____

◆ Write the letter of the figure or figures described on the right.

13. rectangle

16. trapezoid

14. quadrilateral

17. square

15. parallelogram

18. rhombus

a

d

b

e

c

f

◆ Add or subtract.

19. $\frac{4}{5} - \frac{1}{4} =$

20. $\frac{6}{7} - \frac{2}{3} =$

21. $\frac{13}{14} - \frac{8}{9} =$

22. $\frac{3}{5} + \frac{5}{6} =$

23. $\frac{11}{4} - \frac{7}{3} =$

24. $\frac{10}{8} - \frac{2}{7} =$

25. $\frac{3}{7} + \frac{5}{9} =$

26. $\frac{3}{8} + \frac{2}{7} =$

27. $1\frac{2}{4} + 3\frac{3}{8} =$

Bonus Box:
Write a message in a number code for a classmate to solve. Remember to include the key so it can be solved!

◆ Find the missing integer.

1. -65 - -21 = _____

2. -33 - -2 = _____

3. -75 - -10 = _____

4. 87 - 15 = _____

5. 19 - -5 = _____

6. -43 - 7 = _____

7. 17 - -4 = _____

8. -14 - -6 = _____

9. -27 - -9 = _____

10. -46 - -24 = _____

11. 95 - -76 = _____

12. -8 - -3 = _____

◆ Find the circumference. Use 3.14 for π.

13.

41 mm

14.

37 mm

15.

28 mm

◆ Daily ticket sales: 73, 65, 68, 49, 57, 59, 63, 67, 65, 52, 65

Find the:

16. range _____

17. median _____

18. mode _____

19. mean _____

Bonus Box:
Write a message using a shape code for a classmate to solve. Remember to include the key so it can be solved!

Name _____

◆ Find the missing integer.

1. 44 - 54 = _____

2. 83 - 71 = _____

3. 69 - 57 = _____

4. 59 - 43 = _____

5. 24 - 18 = _____

6. -11 - 9 = _____

7. 10 - 7 = _____

8. 8 - 3 = _____

9. 14 - 5 = _____

10. 17 - 8 = _____

11. 69 - 32 = _____

12. 24 - 14 = _____

◆ Find the area. Use 3.14 for π.

13.

21 mm

14.

28 mm

15.

40 mm

◆ Determine the variable.

16. $4x = 44$

17. $x - 17 = 48$

18. $\dfrac{z}{4} = 27$

19. $t + 15 = 37$

20. $7n = 16.1$

21. $w - 21 = 98$

22. $\dfrac{z}{2.5} = 18.75$

23. $r + 8.3 = 13.5$

24. $4.5x = 74.25$

Bonus Box:

If you have three different pairs of jeans and five different sweatshirts, how many different outfits can you make? Use drawings to give your answer.

◆ Find the missing integer.

1. $-4 \cdot -3 =$ _____

2. $-14 \cdot 5 =$ _____

3. $4 \cdot 7 =$ _____

4. $-30 \cdot 12 =$ _____

5. $-20 \cdot -9 =$ _____

6. $-17 \cdot -6 =$ _____

7. $3 \cdot -17 =$ _____

8. $-7 \cdot -6 =$ _____

9. $-34 \cdot 0 =$ _____

10. $14 \cdot -18 =$ _____

11. $13 \cdot -25 =$ _____

12. $-11 \cdot -13 =$ _____

◆ Identify each pair of angle as vertical angles, corresponding angles, or supplementary angles.

13. $\angle 7$ and $\angle 2$ 17. $\angle 7$ and $\angle 5$

14. $\angle 5$ and $\angle 4$ 18. $\angle 3$ and $\angle 1$

15. $\angle 4$ and $\angle 6$ 19. $\angle 1$ and $\angle 7$

16. $\angle 7$ and $\angle 1$ 20. $\angle 3$ and $\angle 4$

◆ Find the equivalent for x.

21. $\dfrac{4}{5} = \dfrac{9}{x}$

22. $\dfrac{x}{7} = \dfrac{9}{18}$

23. $\dfrac{5}{x} = \dfrac{7}{21}$

24. $\dfrac{8}{11} = \dfrac{x}{22}$

25. $\dfrac{x}{15} = \dfrac{45}{135}$

26. $\dfrac{8}{x} = \dfrac{12}{120}$

27. $\dfrac{18}{24} = \dfrac{12}{x}$

28. $\dfrac{9}{x} - = \dfrac{8}{112}$

29. $\dfrac{3}{5} = \dfrac{x}{10}$

Bonus Box:
Ask at least eight other people what their favorite season is. Then construct a line graph on which to display your data.

Answer Key

Page 1

1. 11,987
2. 99.81
3. 789.86
4. 26901
5. 14734.57
6. 15846
7. 26.51
8. 151,440
9. 10,811.95
10. 63.23

11a. 24 in.
 b. 36 in.
 c. 22 in.
12. $.60
13. $.70
14. $2.94
15. $.69
16. $.82
17. $2.04
18. $1.17

Bonus Box: Any shape divided in 10 equal pieces with three of them colored in

Page 2

1. 5,036
2. 70.5
3. 1,004
4. 532
5. 1.8
6. 23.43
7. 158.93
8. 91.6

9. 4.84
10. 13.24
11. 429.35
12. 13.77
13. a. 24 in.
 b. 24 in.
 c. 18 in.

Possible answers:

14. 3 quarters, 1 nickel, 3 pennies
15. 3 quarters, 1 dime, 1 nickel, 4 pennies
16. 1 quarter, 2 pennies
17. 2 quarters, 1 dime, 1 nickel, 2 pennies
18. 1 quarter, 1 dime, 1 penny

Bonus Box: Proofs will vary. May use rulers, existing 90° corners in room, etc.

Page 3

1. 124.747
2. 1,423
3. 146.61
4. 1,508.795
5. 2,330.459
6. 4,785.388
7. 80.715
8. 79.17
9. 100.183
10. 31.488
11. 564.125
12. 998.466

13.a. 7 in.
 b. 8 in.
 c. 9 in.
14. 36 in.
15. 54 in.
16. 24 in.
17. 84 in.
18. 54 in.
19. 234 in.
20. 29 in.
21. 49 in.
22. 245 in.

Page 4

1. 298.68
2. 697
3. 6.886
4. 977
5. 0.673
6. 13.432
7. 459.84
8. 80.995

9. 22.07
10. 6.459
11. 82.24
12. a. 8 in. b. 5 in. c. 3 in.
13. 12:50 P.M.
14. 1 hr, 45 min.
15. 1:35
16. 8:46 P.M.

Bonus Box: answers will vary.

Page 5

1. 2,112
2. 2.925
3. 9.422
4. 5.997
5. 248
6. 6,272
7. 1.305
8. 72.51
9. 97.209
10. 641.167
11. 36.46
12. 4.84
13. acute

14. acute
15. obtuse
16. 45,000
17. 1,000
18. 4,000
19. 35,000
20. 1,000
21. 16,000
22. 10,000
23. 60,000
24. 100,000
25. 1,000
26. 146,000
27. 14,000

Page 6

1. 3,402
2. 6,804
3. 72,032
4. 423,010
5. 29,358
6. 5,602,576
7. 26,052
8. 335,013
9. 101,276
10. 39,402

11. 0.67, 3/4, 7/6, 1.3, 4/3
12. 1/2, 0.75, 1.2, 8/3, 6.7
13. 0.6, 5/7, 3/4, 0.9, 9/7
14. 0.2, 0.5, 2/3, 5/6, 9/10
15. 2/8, 3/9, 0.4, 4/6, 0.74
16. 1/9, 3/10, 0.7, 0.8, 6/5
17. 23
18. 20
19. 35
20. 19

Page 7

1. 2,100
2. 25,704
3. 33,855
4. 3,073,620
5. 8,480,904
6. 2,721,924
7. 6,270,862
8. 3,205,696
9. 2,043,716
10. 1,294,839
11. 35 square inches

12. 27 square inches
13. 49 square inches
14. 6
15. 19
16. 5
17. 54
18. 79
19. 90
20. 91
21. 66
22. 80

Page 8

1. 203,612
2. 854,784
3. 561,681
4. 4,640,532
5. 1,388,220
6. 43,139,352
7. 23,842,962
8. 30,541,664
9. 55,791,153
10. 23,824,295
11. 1
12. 1
13. 6

14. 4
15. 3
16. 11.4
17. 3.0
18. 1.5
19. 3.0
20. 5.3
21. 1, 2, 4, 5, 10, 20
22. 1, 3, 5, 15
23. 1, 2, 3, 6, 9, 18
24. 1, 2, 3, 5, 6, 10, 15, 30
25. 1, 3, 7, 21
26. 1, 3, 9

Bonus Box: 9 ways, 2 dimes
1 dime, 2 nickels
4 nickels
20 pennies
5 pennies, 1 dime, 1 nickel
5 pennies, 3 nickels
10 pennies, 1 dime
10 pennies, 2 nickels
15 pennies, 1 nickel

Page 9

1. 155.94
2. 34.08
3. 485.6
4. 36.4
5. 136.35
6. 2,554.74
7. 3,854.9
8. 30,004.2
9. 7,583.28
10. 5,271
11. 2 x 3 x 31
12. 2 x 2 x 2 x 7 or 2^3 x 7
13. 2 x 2 x 2 x 3 x 5 or 2^3 x 3 x 5
14. 1,143
15. 17,745
16. 2,995,667
17. 105,924
18. 4,337,701

Page 10

1. 2,114.154
2. 7,326
3. 11,175.165
4. 15,078.8
5. 601,471.87
6. 5,484
7. 747.73
8. 27,097.224
9. 3,384.288
10. 170.872
11. 18 inches
12. 42 inches
13. 2 1/2 or 2.5 feet
14. 5 feet
15. 3 1/2 or 3.5 feet
16. 51 inches
17. 18 1/3 yards
18. 6 2/3 yards
19. 25
20. 343
21. 64
22. 512
23. 81
24. 625
25. 27
26. 32
27. 216

Bonus Box: $3.16 change: 3 ones, 1 dime, 1 nickel, 1 penny

Page 11

1. 330.0102
2. 55.848856
3. 42.223094
4. 259.7802
5. 100.56354
6. 11.36592
7. 1.1735
8. 17.2024
9. 122.4816
10. 3.43368
11. 1
12. 5
13. 0
14. 1
15. 1
16. 5
17. 3
18. 2
19. 5
20. 15
21. 24
22. 4
23. 20
24. 30
25. 6
26. 12
27. 42
28. 40
29. 9

Bonus Box: 300,000 + 60,000 + 5,000 + 400 + 20 + 1
50,000 + 9,000 + 40 + 2

Page 12

1. .01935
2. .00192
3. .82152
4. .218268
5. .59724
6. .0273
7. .074304
8. .400113
9. .351864
10. .119695

Primes: 2, 3, 5, 7, 11, 13, 17, 19, 23
11. 1 hour, 45 minutes
12. 4 hours, 25 minutes

Page 13

1. 44.7928
2. 6,039.4382
3. 1,543.5584
4. 381.2055
5. 1,694.1016
6. 5.6869
7. 64.26044
8. 102.79704
9. 41.56296
10. 278.60058
11. 32, 64, 128 (x 2)
12. 46, 94, 190 (x2 + 2)
13. 82, 73, 62 (-1, -3, -5, . . .)
14. 50, 98, 194 (x 2 -2)
15. 1 + 3 + 5 + 7 + 9 + 7 + 5 + 3 + 1
    1 + 3 + 5 + 7 + 9 + 11 + 9 + 7 + 5 + 3 + 1
    1 + 3 + 5 + 7 + 9 + 11 + 13 + 11 + 9 + 7 + 5 + 3 + 1
16. 1/2
17. 3/4
18. 1/3
19. 1/4
20. 2/3
21. 1/7
22. 1/4
23. 1/7

Page 14

1. 161.0105
2. 26.929271
3. 53,207.864
4. 46,440,044
5. 1.0480613
6. 2,236.5798
7. 1,451.6
8. 7,524
9. 5,083,175
10. 0.16206
11. 18 square inches
12. 12 square inches
13. 40 square inches
14. 5 square inches
15. 7.96
16. 49,648
17. 17.6
18. 119.03
19. 1,068.04
20. 1,626.1
21. 85,381
22. 434
23. 80,603.5474
24. 61

Page 15

1. 266,445
2. 319,914
3. 0.000015
4. 3,042
5. 2,172.1856
6. 2.02644
7. 36.728
8. 603,848
9. 34,905
10. 111.2454
11. 4
12. 4
13. 3
14. 2
15. 5
16. 10
17. 2
18. 2
19. 3
20. 1
21. 4
22. 1

triangular number: 36

Page 16

1. 58r4
2. 19
3. 60 r3
4. 244 r4
5. 713 r3
6. 451 r 5
7. 1,369 r3
8. 8,774 r2
9. 5,629 r6
10. 4,175 r6
11. 8
12. 23
13. 33
14. 100
15. 8
16. 765
17. 22
18. 37
19. 100
20. 235,874,900
21. 236,000,000
22. 235,875,000
23. 235,870,000
24. 235,900,000

Bonus Box: one possible solution 6 x 107

Page 17

1. 3 r 16
2. 3 r9
3. 11 r57
4. 108 r4
5. 20 r 27
6. 29 r9
7. 94 r2
8. 91 r1
9. 14 r24
10. 88 r11
11. 12
12. 30
13. 12
14. 60
15. 30
16. 42
17. 24
18. 18
19. 60
20. 20 oz.
21. 35 oz.
22. 4 lb.
23. 2 1/2 lbs.
24. 71 1/4 lbs.
25. 1,760 oz.

Page 18

1. 171 r26
2. 33 r2
3. 13 r28
4. 300 r2
5. 206 r4
6. 204 r36
7. 970 r6
8. 86 r2
9. 60 r38
10. 119 r30

5 squared: 25

• • • • •
• • • • •
• • • • •
• • • • •
• • • • •

possible squares greater than 95:
100, 121, 144

11. 300
12. 150
13. 8
14. 60
15. 635
16. 250
17. 34,500
18. 1/2 or .5
19. 5
20. 2,500

Page 19

1. 2 r89
2. 106 r123
3. 43 r1
4. 71 r56
5. 171 r50
6. 32 r 79
7. 84 r72
8. 108 r41
9. 52 square inches
10. 110 square inches
11. 45 square inches

12.–15. Students may find other patterns that will work.

12. 122 (x3 - 1)
13. 94 (x2 +2)
14. 78 (-5)
15. 61 (x2 + 3)

Page 20

1. 876
2. 1,303.3
3. 2,830
4. 674.2
5. 716.2
6. 26,143.3
7. 13,127.5
8. 12,937.1
9. 15,011.6
10. 8,973.3
11. 2
12. 9
13. 9
14. 7
15. 9
16. 5
17. 1
18. 4
19. 6
20. 10
21. $3.22 Possible change: three $1 bills 2 dimes, 2 pennies
22. $7.87 Possible change: one $5 bill, two $1 bills, three quarters, one dime, two pennies
23. $7.15 Possible change: one $5 bill, two $1 bills, one dime, one nickel

Page 21

1. 2,713.0
2. 72.5
3. 7,563.6
4. 87,933.3
5. 703.7
6. 23.8
7. 442.8
8. 105.0
9. 4,686.6
10. 895.5
11. 9
12. 7
13. 7
14. 4
15. 6
16. 4
17. 36 in.
18. 32 in.
19. 35 in.
20. 26 in.

Bonus Box: One easy way to do this is use a string for the outline and then measure the string.

Page 22

1. 227.4
2. 47,723.6
3. 203.7
4. 5,392.5
5. 2,875
6. 666.6
7. 17.0
8. 120.0
9. 164
10. 991.9
11. $2 \times 2 \times 17$ or $2^2 \times 17$
12. $2 \times 2 \times 23$ or $2^2 \times 23$ or $2 \times 2 \times 2 \times 2 \times 7$ or $2^4 \times 7$
13. 5×47
14. 16,168
15. 619,605
16. 7,518,784
17. 7,061,094
18. 17,505
19. 130,448
20. 875,124
21. 52,206

Bonus Box: one possible problem $285 \div 3$

Page 23

1. 46.743
2. .0528
3. 5.24
4. .03008
5. 21.385
6. 5.2237
7. .06
8. .427
9. .653
10. 3.8297
11. 2.281
12. .0168
13. 72 cu. in.
14. 32 cu. in.
15. 96 cu. in.
16. 54 cu. in.
17. 2 1/3, 12 1/2, 13.42, 14.2, 67.4
18. 6.49, 6 7/14, 6 3/4, 7 1/10, 7.25
19. 5.2, 5 1/4, 5.3, 5 6/8, 5.8
20. 2.1, 2 1/4, 2.7, 2 3/4, 2.8

Bonus Box: 13 different ways

1. 1 quarter
2. 2 dimes, 1 nickel
3. 1 dime, 3 nickels
4. 5 nickels
5. 2 dimes, 5 pennies
6. 1 dime, 15 pennies
7. 1 nickel, 20 pennies
8. 2 nickels, 15 pennies
9. 3 nickels, 10 pennies
10. 4 nickels, 5 pennies
11. 25 pennies
12. 1 dime, 1 nickel, 10 pennies
13. 1 dime, 2 nickels, 5 pennies

Page 24

1. 2
2. 4.58
3. .75
4. .071
5. 4.1
6. 750
7. 67.5
8. 11.86
9. 13.07
10. 3.62
11. 3/4
12. 5/6
13. 7/9
14. 2/3
15. 3/4
16. 3/5
17. 6/7
18. 5/6
19. 108
20. 50
21. 200
22. 17
23. 41 r2
24. 4
25. 20
26. 16

Page 25

1.	3.1	9.	69.6
2.	341	10.	781.2
3.	.77	11.	44.8
4.	.49	12.	77.83
5.	20.9	13.	94.6
6.	9	14.	79.3
7.	9.5	15.	74.5
8.	5.2	16.	12

17. 49, 64, 81 (square numbers)
18. 75, 45, 10 (-1, -10, -15, . . .)
19. 364, 1093, 3280 (x 3, +1)
20. 34, 55, 89 (add the two previous numbers together.)

Page 26

1.	15.2	16.	.5
2.	1.5	17.	2/10 or 1/5
3.	51.4	18.	9/100
4.	9.9	19.	.75
5.	.29	20.	2/10 or 1/5
6.	1.3	21.	.3
7.	69.0	22.	83/100
8.	35	23.	28.67
9.	60	24.	197.2
10.	1.9	25.	262.08
11.	0.4	26.	0.21744
12.	.09	27.	9.672
13.	75/100 or 3/4	28.	0.247
14.	0.25	29.	18.834
15.	6/10 or 3/5	30.	1434.72

Page 27

1.	6 r4	12.	2/6, 3/6
2.	47 r5	13.	9/15, 4/15
3.	2 r52	14.	6/9, 1/9
4.	87 r6	15.	15/21, 7/21
5.	7 r 67	16.	2/9, 6/9
6.	10 r 314	17.	6/30, 5/30
7.	2 r 41	18.	10/35, 14/35
8.	142 r5	19.	3/18, 4/18
9.	15 r30	20.	3:20
10.	4	21.	8 hours, 20 minutes
11.	4/12, 3/12	22.	2 hours, 15 minutes

Page 28

1.	63.2	11.	123,500
2.	1,127.5	12.	123,456.988
3.	5.89	13.	120,000
4.	0.122	14.	123,456.9877
5.	9,450	15.	8
6.	420.6	16.	3
7.	753.3	17.	4
8.	135.3	18.	8.5 or 8 1/2
9.	178.3	19.	2
10.	155.0	20.	3.5 or 3 1/2

Page 29

1.	1.2	11.	60 sq. in.
2.	23.78	12.	64 sq. in.
3.	.326	13.	80 sq. in.
4.	64.1	14.	7,057
5.	10.8	15.	127
6.	.208	16.	6.3
7.	.659	17.	108
8.	192.8	18.	828.644
9.	62	19.	41,976
10.	82	20.	138,653

Page 30

1.	16.097	15.	6
2.	8.63	16.	72
3.	1,325.8	17.	12
4.	1.2	18.	9
5.	.93	19.	15
6.	4.5	20.	10
7.	8.55	21.	21
8.	5.80	22.	18
9.	2,102.5	23.	64
10.	18	24.	64
11.	30	25.	10
12.	14	26.	5
13.	24	27.	1 1/2
14.	40	28.	4

Page 31

1.	1/2	13.	1/3
2.	2/3	14.	1/6
3.	3/4	15.	3/4
4.	4/5	16.	3/4
5.	2/3	17.	4/5
6.	5/7	18.	2/7
7.	10/11	19.	1/5
8.	7/9	20.	2/9
9.	7/8	21.	1/8
10.	4/5	22.	1/2
11.	1/2	23.	3/7
12.	1/3	24.	1/4
		25.	8/9

26. $5.44, one $5 bill, one quarter, one dime, one nickel, four pennies
27. $1.71, one $1 bill, two quarters, two dimes, one penny
28. 41¢, four dimes, one penny

Page 32

1.	3/4	12.	32
2.	1 1/4	13.	10
3.	2/3	14.	75
4.	1 1/3	15.	9
5.	2/3	16.	20
6.	1 2/11	17.	17
7.	1/2	18.	50
8.	1 2/7	19.	7.5
9.	1 1/4	20.	1 1/4 or 1.25
10.	1 1/9	21.	1,680
11.	22	22.	10

Page 33

1.	7/12	15.	1 1/4
2.	3/8	16.	1 1/2
3.	13/15	17.	1 1/2
4.	11/30	18.	2 1/4
5.	7/10	19.	3
6.	13/20	20.	1 1/3
7.	4/9	21.	1 2/7
8.	3/8	22.	4 2/3
9.	4/9	23.	2 1/2
10.	15/28	24.	4 1/4
11.	2 1/5	25.	5
12.	3 3/5	26.	1 hour, 30 minutes
13.	6 1/3	27.	5 hours, 30 minutes
14.	1 1/5	28.	No, in 48 minutes

Page 34
1. 29/35
2. 46/63
3. 11/24
4. 7/10
5. 3/4
6. 11/18
7. 5/14
8. 13/15
9. 9/10
10. 7/18
11. 6
12. 3 1/2
13. 4 3/4
14. 6 1/2
15. 6 1/3
16. 5 2/3
17. 8 1/2
18. 3 1/8
19. 3 1/4
20. 7 1/2
21. 11
22. 6 3/4
23. 8 1/7
24. 6 4/5
25. 14 1/3
Students may find other patterns to arrive at the correct numbers.
26. 28, 36 (triangular numbers)
27. 64, 128 (double numbers)
28. 243, 729 (x3)
29. 42, 49 (multiples of 7)
30. 31, 43 (+2, +4, +6, ...)
31. 3125, 15,625

Page 35
1. 1 7/15
2. 1 4/15
3. 1 1/4
4. 1 7/45
5. 1 2/9
6. 1 1/18
7. 1 7/18
8. 1 1/22
9. 1 5/9
10. 1 8/21
11. 9 sq. units
12. 8 sq. units
13. 8 1/2 sq. units
14. 10 sq. units
15. 3,204
16. 603,978
17. 38,660,876
18. 104,598
19. 16,986
20. 2,962,338
21. 2,035,028
22. 3,766,290

Page 36
1. 4 1/6
2. 7 1/2
3. 7 11/40
4. 13 5/21
5. 8 1/8
6. 10 7/12
7. 7 11/63
8. 12 17/42
9. 13 1/6
10. 7 1/10
11.
12.
13.
14. 21.5
15. 36
16. 3.5
17. 10
18. 20
19. 14

Page 37
1. 5/6
2. 4/5
3. 9/11
4. 3/4
5. 2/3
6. 8/9
7. 5/6
8. 4/5
9. 5/7
10. 3/4
11. 192 cu. in.
12. 96 cu. in.
13. 70 cu. in.
14. 78 r6
15. 23 r 15
16. 8 r 49
17. 51 r1
18. 8 r 744
19. 4 r11
20. 54 r7
21. 2 r 15

Page 38
1. 1 4/5
2. 1 1/2
3. 1 1/16
4. 1 3/4
5. 2 1/5
6. 1 7/10
7. 1 5/18
8. 2 1/3
9. 1 4/25
10. 1 3/10
11-13 Drawings will vary.
14. 2,089
15. 2,041
16. 384
17. 10,004
18. 104,919
19. 63
20. 757,575

Page 39
1. 5/6
2. 3/4
3. 11/20
4. 11/14
5. 13/18
6. 9/10
7. 19/24
8. 41/44
9. 33/40
10. 14/15
11. 8
12. 6
13. 99.5
14. 170
15. 17
16. 46
17. 96
18. 34
19. 60
20. two quarters; five dimes; one quarter, two dimes, and one nickel
21. three quarters; seven dimes, one nickel; one half-dollar, one quarter
22. one half-dollar, one dime; two quarters, and one dime; six dimes
23. eight dimes; three quarters, one nickel; one half-dollar, one quarter, one nickel
21.-23. Other combinations are possible.

Page 40
1. 31/36
2. 3/4
3. 11/21
4. 2/3
5. 13/20
6. 95/126
7. 17/24
8. 13/60
9. 15/28
10. 9/20
14. 0.646
15. 2.4336
16. 20.4792
17. 298.52
18. 1.3158
19. 105.2532
20. 1.71152
21. 33.7483
11., 12., 13. congruent shapes are exactly the same

Page 41
1. 2
2. 1 27/40
3. 1 34/63
4. 1 5/9
5. 1 1/6
6. 1 11/24
7. 1 11/21
8. 1 13/24
9. 1 21/44
10. 1 11/24
11. 2.5 sq. units
12. 12 sq. units
13. 9 sq. units
14. 9 sq. units
15. 10
16. 3,650
17. 168
18. 1,440
19. 30.4
20. 30

Page 42

1. 12 29/30
2. 13 2/3
3. 15 7/10
4. 17 27/28
5. 13 5/8
6. 17 1/2
7. 8 22/63
8. 9 9/70
9. 11 23/33
10. 17 23/72
11. 2 x 2 x 2 x 7 x 3
    2^3 x 7 x 3

12. 2 x 2 x 5 x 5
    2^2 x 5^2
13. 2 x 2 x 2 x 5 x 5
    2^3 x 5^2
14. 3.4
15. 0.712
16. 3937.3
17. 3.2
18. .001
19. 1.8
20. 20.1
21. 5.57

Page 43

1. 7 7/60
2. 16 13/36
3. 10 13/15
4. 10 7/12
5. 8 11/30
6. 15 3/5
7. 14 77/78
8. 14 1/5
9. 22 7/45
10. 22 53/56
11.

12. [pentagon figure]
13. [hexagon figure]
14. 7,000
15. 6
16. 2,500
17. 10.5
18. 2.75
19. 32,000

Page 44

1. 1 5/12
2. 1 3/7
3. 10 4/5
4. 10 7/12
5. 1 41/45
6. 1 1/2
13. 35 cu. in.

15. [triangle figure]

7. 7/8
8. 1 13/36
9. 17 3/5
10. 1 28/45
11. 108 cu. in.
12. 60 cu. in.
14.

16. [circle and square figures]

Page 45

1. 1 4/5
2. 9 7/9
3. 10 2/5
4. 2 1/4
5. 7 1/2
6. 2 11/36
7. 19 37/72
8. 4
9. 1 1/2
10. 14 3/28

11. 7
12. 52
13. 2
14. 156
15. 55
16. 14
17. 5,280
18. 15
19. 8.5
20. 144
21. 294

Page 46

1. 1/4
2. 1/3
3. 3/7
4. 2/5
5. 1/2
6. 1/11
7. 1/3
8. 1/3
9. 1/3
10. 2/9
11. 1/2
12. 1/2

13. 3/4
14. 2/3
15. 2/3
16. 3/5
17. 2/5
18. 1/2
19. 3/5
20. 4/5
21. 2/3
22. 1/4
23. 1 minute, 45 seconds
24. 1 hour, 45 minutes
25. 3 P.M., 10 P.M.

Bonus Box: 6 handshakes

Page 47

1. 6 1/2
2. 7 1/4
3. 3 5/12
4. 8 2/5
5. 7 4/9
6. 9 2/3
7. 2 1/4
8. 13 2/3
9. 4 4/15
10. 7 1/8
11. 1 3/8
12. 1 2/3
13. 1 2/15
14. 1 1/2
Bonus: 6

15. 3 1/2
16. 2 2/3
17. 2 1/2
18. 2 1/3
19. 4
20. 2 5/6
21. 4 3/4
22. 2 1/3
23. 9.5
24. 24 ounces
25. 36
26. 5
27. 32 ounces
28. 4

Page 48

1. 11 4/5
2. 7 14/19
3. 4 2/3
4. 14 5/6
5. 6 1/4
6. 31 5/8
7. 2 2/3
8. 9 7/12
9. 1/3
10. 3 1/4
11. 1,728
12. 27

13. 1.5 or 1 1/2
14. 3
15. 46,656
16. 3
17. 14,670
18. 43,488
19. 623
20. 2,338,560
21. 87,912
22. 11,128
23. 46,800
24. 4,368,384

Page 49

1. 3 2/5
2. 5 5/9
3. 4 3/7
4. 7 5/6
5. 2 1/3
6. 3 2/3
7. 4 1/2
8. 8 1/4
9. 2 7/9
10. 4/5
11. 36

12. 50
13. 200
14. 17
15. 41 2/3
16. 4
17. 20
18. 16
19. 40
20. $1.21 one $1 bill, 2 dimes, 1 penny
21. $1.24, one $1 bill, 2 dimes, 4 pennies
22. 77¢ 3 quarters, 2 pennies

Page 50

1. 2 2/7
2. 2 1/2
3. 3 3/5
4. 3/5
5. 2 5/9
6. 5 8/15
7. 2 3/16
8. 1 1/5
9. 1 1/2
10. 1/2
11. 6 sq. units
12. 5 sq. units
13. 13 sq. units
14. 9 sq. units
15. 99,409
16. 3,811
17. 174,914
18. 2,513
19. 77,163

Page 51

1. 5/12
2. 19/36
3. 8/15
4. 13/25
5. 1/2
6. 5/14
7. 13/16
8. 20/39
9. 1/2
10. 5/12
11.
12. ∨
13. @
14.
15. 7
16. 13
17. 28
18. 15
19. 8
20. 20

Page 52

1. 3/25
2. 2/5
3. 11/18
4. 9/35
5. 1/3
6. 1/6
7. 2/5
8. 19/40
9. 8/35
10. 1/12
Bonus: 10
11. Students could check each other's work.
12. Students could check each other's work.
13. Students could check each other's work.\
14. 0.3521
15. 229.307
16. 0.033056
17. 237.63
18. 43.008
19. 10.918
20. 35.131
21. 6.494

Page 53

1. 1/100
2. 1/15
3. 2/9
4. 3/14
5. 1/12
6. 1/8
7. 1/18
8. 1/6
9. 1/18
10. 1/6
11.
12.
13.
14. 6 inches
15. 3/4
16. 10 feet

Page 54

1. 6 5/8
2. 2 17/36
3. 8 9/40
4. 4 17/70
5. 10/21
6. 6 1/2
7. 7 16/63
8. 1 9/10
9. 3 41/45
10. 2 5/6
11. 25
12. 26
13. 43
14. 50
15. 70
16. 50
17. 4 1/4
18. 5 5/8
19. 3 1/2
20. 12 2/9
21. 10 3/5
22. 9 4/7
23. 4 2/3
24. 9 2/5

Page 55

1. 4 25/72
2. 1 11/60
3. 4 2/5
4. 8 1/3
5. 6 7/16
6. 5/6
7. 5 47/70
8. 7 7/8
9. 2 25/34
10. 8 7/18
11. 210 sq. in.
12. 49.875 sq. in.
13. 150 sq. in.
14. 2 r 19
15. 375 r3
16. 9 r48
17. 122 r10
18. 69
19. 146 r6
20. 115 r63
21. 4 r 150

Page 56

1. 1 7/9
2. 4 5/18
3. 5 1/2
4. 4 7/24
5. 1 2/5
6. 1 29/39
7. 1 19/20
8. 2 10/21
9. 4 17/30
10. 5/12
11. m ∈ ω
12. ▶ ◥
13. ◉ ◉ ◉
14. 9 P.M.
15. possible answers: 4:00, 8:00, 10:30

Page 57

1. 1 12/35
2. 3 21/40
3. 1 11/30
4. 3 7/18
5. 2 21/55
6. 2 14/45
7. 7 17/48
8. 2 17/50
9. 1 12/35
10. 3 29/56
11. Shapes will vary.
12. Shapes will vary.
13. Shapes will vary.
14. 1,000
15. 6,400
16. 450
17. 99.5
18. 4.5
19. 100,000

Bonus Box: 24 different ways

Page 58

1. 1 4/9
2. 1/2
3. 5 11/24
4. 1 1/2
5. 13/21
6. 2 5/9
7. 3 2/5
8. 3/5
9. 1 3/8
10. 23/100
11. 55, 65, 75 (+10)
12. 127, 255, 511 (2^x - 1) or (+2, +4, +8 . . . .)
13. 106, 141, 181 (+5, +10, + 15, . . .)
14. 7, 1, 7 (+6, -6, +6, =6, . . .)
15. 157.8
16. 16.6
17. 463
18. 1,123.9
19. 4.25
20. 7,303.3
21. 30.24
22. 9.81

Page 59

1. 1 /72
2. 1 11/12
3. 3 4/9
4. 2 3/28
5. 4 4/5
6. 3 17/40
7. 1 16/21
8. 4 2/3
9. 3 1/6
10. 4 9/20
11. 10
12. 70
13. 70
14. 48.4
15. 45
16. 1,500
17. 1 1/4
18. 1 8/35
19. 1 7/36
20. 1 1/10
21. 6 11/12
22. 1 1/8
23. 8 3/5
24. 8 9/35

© Instructional Fair • TS Denison

118

IF87124 Mixed Skills in Math

Page 60
1. 1 25/28
2. 1 14/45
3. 1 1/3
4. 2/5
5. 5/48
6. 2 1/10
7. 7/24
8. 4 20/21
9. 1 4/9
10. 1/3
11. <
12. ⟷
13. ▭
14. 1 dime, 4 nickels
15. 1 half dollar, 1 quarter, 1 dime, 1 nickel
16. 1 quarter, 2 dimes, 5 pennies

Page 61
1. 2/15
2. 1/8
3. 2/15
4. 10/21
5. 21/40
6. 7/20
7. 3/16
8. 1/20
9. 8/21
10. 4/27
11. 6/35
12. 1/8
13. $11.95
14. 15.2 (also 1.52)
15. $3.95
16. 23.5
17. $4.50, $2.75
18. 1 29/30
19. 7 1/8
20. 2 1/9
21. 1 1/6
22. 2 17/72
23. 2 19/42
24. 5 7/15
25. 43/44

Page 62
1. 7/16
2. 24/55
3. 5/44
4. 3/56
5. 2/27
6. 25/42
7. 16/35
8. 8/45
9. 8/81
10. 1/6
11. 15/32
12. 6/35
13. -2° C
14. -3° C
15. 25° C
16. 80° C
17. 5.5
18. 4.75
19. 75.5
20. 75.2
21. 96.5
22. 84.3

Page 63
1. 1/3
2. 1/3
3. 2/11
4. 1 2/3
5. 3
6. 5/8
7. 1/5
8. 1/10
9. 3/5
10. 1/10
11. 5/12
12. 1/4

possible answers:
13. 1/4, 5/20, 2/8
14. 2/3, 4/6, 6/9
15. 2/3, 4/6, 6/9
16. 1/2, 2/4, 3/6
17. 1/3, 2/6, 3/9
18. 61 r7
19. 93 r29
20. 49.3
21. 2,725.8
22. 307 r1
23. 11,600
24. .00008
25. 15.9

Page 64
1. 9/35
2. 5/32
3. 2/3
4. 5/12
5. 2
6. 10
7. 1/10
8. 3/5
9. 3/10
10. 2/5
11. 7/11
12. 1/4
13. 180
14. 150
15. 2
16. 84
17. 2
18. 1.5
19. 1.5
20. 3
21. 54,090,000
22. 5,395,300
23. 13,000
24. 56,395.6683

Page 65
1. 45 5/8
2. 41 17/24
3. 25 5/9
4. 10 5/9
5. 26 1/8
6. 11 2/5
7. 18 1/3
8. 22 1/6
9. 32 3/28
10. 23 7/30
11. 45 1/2
12. 26 3/5
13. ▱
14. ⬭
15. ◹
16. 94,706
17. 588
18. 8,335
19. 10,126
20. 34,065
21. 1,080
22. 63
23. 3,659

Page 66
1. 12 4/15
2. 32 16/25
3. 22 8/63
4. 15 11/36
5. 29 3/4
6. 50 7/20
7. 54 5/8
8. 36 7/8
9. 18 23/28
10. 28 25/54
11. 52 20/27
12. 12 1/10
13. 2 x 2 x 2 x 37 or 2^3 x 37
14. 2 x 2 x 37 or 2^2 x 37
15. 2 x 5 x 7
16. 122.08
17. 31.9456
18. 5.5289
19. 45,108
20. 2,660
21. 244,080
22. 15,127.18
23. 129.26

Page 67
1. 2/7
2. 2 13/16
3. 5 1/3
4. 6 3/16
5. 7 11/15
6. 6
7. 10/21
8. 1/4
9. 4
10. 2 5/6
11. 29 4/9
12. 31 1/2
13. 16 sq. units
14. 8 sq. units
15. 10 sq. units
16. 12
17. 60
18. 28
19. 30
20. 18
21. 44
22. 40
23. 30
24. 24

Page 68
1. 3
2. 36 1/9
3. 7 13/20
4. 3/4
5. 3 1/3
6. 9/16
7. 5 5/14
8. 19
9. 2/3
10. 6 2/5
11. 32 2/3
12. 2/3
13. acute
14. obtuse
15. right
16. acute
17. 1 7/20
18. 1/2
19. 1 3/8
20. 9 41/45
21. 1 7/18
22. 5 15/56
23. 2 3/5
24. 26/63

Page 69
1. 8/1
2. 4/3
3. 5/2
4. 9/2
5. 3/2
6. 7/3
7. 5/4
8. 5/1
9. 10/2
10. 8/3
11. 144
12. 22
13. 3
14. 4 1/3
15. 3 1/12
16. 56
17. 13, 2
18. 30
19. 9 3/4
20. 3
21. 6
22. 2
23. 4
24. 8
25. 3
26. 6
27. 5

Page 70
1. 1 1/5
2. 1
3. 5
4. 6 3/7
5. 16 1/2
6. 2/3
7. 2 2/5
8. 7/9
9. 1 1/4
10. 3 3/7
11. 3/4
12. 5/6
13. 5
14. 2
15. 3
16. 2
17. 6
18. 1
19. 4
20. 4
21. 8
22. 23.222
23. 9858
24. 19.106136
25. 7374.01
26. 317.9832
27. 2,878,464

Page 71
1. 5 5/7
2. 5/6
3. 1 11/24
4. 15/16
5. 9/64
6. 1 1/5
7. 1 17/60
8. 6 2/3
9. 20/27
10. 4/45
11. 1 5/16
12. 7 1/5
13. 20
14. 96
15. 7.5
16. 2.5
17. 4
18. 16
19. 3/4
20. 8 3/4
21. 3/8
22. 1 1/4
23. 16
24. 3, 1
25. 10 r19
26. 471.1
27. 213 r 16
28. 505.2
29. .0402
30. 25 r8

Page 72
1. 2
2. 1 5/27
3. 2/3
4. 2/9
5. 4 1/2
6. 4 19/32
7. 1
8. 2 1/2
9. 6
10. 1 1/2
11. 22 1/2
12. 1 1/2
13. acute
14. obtuse
15. right
16. acute
17. 7 1/15
18. 12 1/6
19. 2 4/15
20. 1 43/72
21. 2 17/36
22. 10 7/24
23. 10 13/60
24. 1 14/45

Page 73
1. 4
2. 1
3. 15
4. 14
5. 4/5
6. 1
7. 16
8. 1 1/2
9. 1
10. 2/3
11. 5/8
12. 12
13. Shapes will vary.
14. Shapes will vary.
15. Shapes will vary.
16. 1/2
17. 12/35
18. 1/8
19. 1/3
20. 3/22
21. 1/20
22. 11/15
23. 4/21
24. 2/3

Page 74
1. 2
2. 1 1/4
3. 145/189
4. 2 62/133
5. 2 11/38
6. 1 49/76
7. 1 11/39
8. 24/35
9. 1 19/31
10. 8/9
11. 2 1/2
12. 3 9/58
13. $2 \times 2 \times 5 \times 5$ or $2^2 \times 5^2$
14. $2 \times 2 \times 2 \times 2 \times 3 \times 3$ or $2^4 \times 3^2$
15. $2 \times 5 \times 5 \times 5$ or 2×5^3
16. 7,015
17. 1,577
18. 667
19. 10.94
20. 1.3
21. 108
22. 1,788
23. 1,738

Page 75
1. 1 3/133
2. 1 29/33
3. 1 1/65
4. 4
5. 2 5/14
6. 2 1/42
7. 2 56/117
8. 2 2/31
9. 1 73/75
10. 3 23/25
11. 1 23/49
12. 1 7/32
13. 32,000
14. 4,000
15. 30
16. 7.8
17. 1.44
18. .4
19. .418
20. 8
21. 4,000
22. 32,022
23. 40,491
24. 554.19
25. 16.87125
26. 677,322
27. 57.5094
28. 4.384
29. 2.9104

Page 76
1. 1/2
2. 3/4
3. 10
4. 1 1/2
5. 1
6. 3 17/45
7. 1/2
8. 1 1/9
9. 4 32/35
10. 1 1/11
11. 3 21/26
12. 1 111/224
13. 10
14. 43
15. 30
16. 24
17. 16
18. 21.5
19. 9
20. 6
21. 4
22. 8
23. 6

Page 77

1. 11/2/3
2. 1
3. 1 1/8
4. 20
5. 1 1/2
6. 2 142/153
7. 1 81/95
8. 4 18/35
9. 5/8
10. 1 1/3
11. 3 13/18
12. 9 1/3

possible answers:
13. 3 quarters, 4 pennies
14. 3 dimes, 1 nickel, 3 pennies
15. 3 quarters, 3 nickels, 3 pennies
16. 1 quarter, 4 nickels
17. 11,772
18. 4.7502
19. 100.3978
20. 2,455,806
21. 3.92021
22. 1,836
23. 186,260
24. 482.22

Page 78

1. 0.93
2. 70%
3. 0.75
4. 50%
5. 34%
6. 0.63
7. 900%
8. 0.125
9. 4.5
10. 0.735
11. 54%

12. 150%
13. 345.8
14. 5,873.89
15. 544.8990
16. 7,809.904
17. 55,482,449.338988
18. 26 7/20
19. 34 7/15
20. 15 2/5
21. 8 3/4
22. 27 13/21
23. 37 4/5

Page 79

1. 24/25
2. 1 3/4
3. 50%
4. 1/3
5. 37.5%
6. 8%
7. 1 1/10
8. 40%
9. 1/40
10. 103%
11. 62.5%

12. 2 3/4
13. 11.5 sq. units
14. 12 sq. units
15. 16 sq. units
16. 7/12
17. 1 1/9
18. 11/15
19. 2 2/5
20. 2 9/28
21. 11 1/2
22. 13 19/24
23. 4 49/80

Page 80

1. 75%
2. 50%
3. 150%
4. .2%
5. 25%
6. 5%
7. 30%
8. 20%
9. 33 1/3%
10. 200%
11.-15. acute angles are: AOB, AOC, BOC, COD, DOE, EOF
    obtuse angles are: AOE, BOD, BOE, BOF, COE, COF
    right angles are: AOD, DOF
16. 112 r2
17. 9947.7
18. 1.876
19. 8613.5
20. 1,564 r3
21. 1,086.7

Page 81

1. 50%
2. 10%
3. 150%
4. 12.5%
5. 25%
6. 25%
7. 25%
8. 10%
9. 15%
10. 20%
11. 4
12. 7

13. 20
14. 15
15. 19
16. 5
17. 8
18. 9
19. 8
20. 2.925
21. 65,577
22. 1,281
23. 384
24. 7,328
25. 7,969
26. 2.7

Page 82

1. 68
2. 120
3. 20
4. 240
5. 60
6. 320
7. 120
8. 50
9. 18
10. 200
11. 3/4

12. 900
13. 1/2
14. 1 1/2
15. 3
16. 48
17. 512,000,000
18. 358,937,000
19. 345,830,000
20. 539,300,000
21. 440,000,000
22. 400,000,000

Page 83

1. 280
2. 20
3. 205
4. 1,200
5. 400
6. 75
7. 90
8. 40
9. 160
10. 80
11. 314
12. 1,176
13. 36

14. 7.5
15. 212
16. 11
17. 15
18. 16
19. 45.5
20. 73.8
21. 25
22. 80.7
23. 6.1
24. 65.4
25. 74.3
26. 72.5

Page 84

1. 168
2. 7
3. 6
4. 7.8
5. 5.4
6. 7.5
7. 56
8. 1.5
9. 9
10. 117
11. 26
12. 96
13. 1 1/4
14. 3,520
15. 3,300

16. 3 1/2
17. 2,640
18. 21
19. 60
20. 23
21. 25
22. 7
23. 1 13/21
24. 1 1/4
25. 4 1/2
26. 4 12/35
27. 10 3/5
28. 1 11/18
29. 5/8
30. 1 19/30

Page 85
1. 68
2. 33 1/3%
3. 20
4. 56
5. 216
6. 75
7. 44%
8. 250%
9. 20
10. 600
11. 58, 61, 122 (x 2 + 3 x 2 + 3 . . .)
12. 159, 161, 483 (x 3 + 2 x 3 + 2 . . .)
13. 4,096; 16,384; 65,536 (x 4)
14. 13, 14, 16 (+1, +2, +1, +2 . . .)
15. 74.5
16. 120 r27
17. 112.4
18. 13.22
19. 132 r21
20. 24.92

Page 86
1. 15%
2. 12.5%
3. 120
4. 18
5. 375
6. 75
7. 3
8. 66 2/3%
9. 100
10. 60
11. 19
12. 28
13. 2 1/4
14. 64
15. 14
16. 64
17. 96
18. 1 1/2
19. 9,968
20. 2,785,852
21. 194.0211
22. 28,424
23. 3.33945
24. 9,735
25. 378.368
26. 31,616

Page 87
1. yes
2. no
3. no
4. yes
5. no
6. yes
7. no
8. no
9. yes
10. no
11. no
12. yes
13. Shapes will vary.
14. Shapes will vary.
15. Shapes will vary.
16. 6
17. 56
18. 15
19. 30
20. 18
21. 24
22. 60
23. 30
24. 24

Page 88
1. 9
2. 5
3. 15
4. 55
5. 12
6. 16
7. 12
8. 10
9. 100
10. 4
11. 8
12. 9
13. 8.8
14. 1.314
15. 1.550
16. 6.076
17. 1,300
18. 12,000
19. 2.356
20. .365
21. 19 7/20
22. 10 5/6
23. 4/7
24. 9 31/40
25. 3/5
26. 16 5/7
27. 16 23/27
28. 32 13/16
29. 5/8

Page 89
1. 12
2. 2.7
3. 24
4. 11
5. 470
6. 6
7. 5
8. 12.5
9. 3
10. 42
11. 22.5
12. 15
13. 92
14. 30
15. 10
16. 18
17. 31
18. 20
19. 1 5/16
20. 1 17/63
21. 1 7/18
22. 1 10/21
23. 1 37/40
24. 1 23/27
25. 3 5/9
26. 7 1/25
27. 25/28

Page 90
1. 55 miles
2. 78 beats
3. 28¢
4. 3/4 in.
5. 48 words
6. approx. 17¢
7. 26¢
8. 1,900 calories
9. $4.50
10. $1.35
11. 12.5%, .125
12. 50%, .5
13. 80%, .8
14. 37.5%, .375
15. 75%, .75
16. 25%, .25
17. 90%, .9
18. 10%, .1
19. 80%, .8
20. 11/21
21. 5 4/9
22. 2/5
23. 2/5
24. 5/24
25. 1 1/2
26. 7 3/8
27. 2 3/5
28. 3 4/15

Page 91
1. 1/6
2. 5/6
3. 1/2
4. 5/6
5. 1/6
6. 2/3
7. 1/2
8. 5/6
9. 1/3
10. 1/2
11. 300 sq. mm
12. 144 sq. mm
13. 216 sq. mm
14. 3.42
15. 638.47
16. 375.168
17. 4.8857
18. 984.56
19. 15.896
20. 340.767
21. 1,017.79

Page 92
1. 1/8
2. 3/8
3. 1/4
4. 1/2
5. 1/4
6. 5/8
7. 3/8
8. 3/8
9. 7/8
10. 3/4
11. 60°
12. 50°
13. 45°
14. 3/7
15. 9 5/8
16. 1/2
17. 3/10
18. 11/32
19. 1/5
20. 19 4/5
21. 5/54
22. 8

Page 93
1. 25
2. 37
3. 38
4. 31.75
5. 13
6. 16
7. 19
8. 14
9. .75
10. .75
11. .25
12. .9
13. .125
14. .8
15. .8
16. .2
17. 8
18. 4.8
19. 24
20. 15
21. 9
22. 11.25

Page 94
1. 17
2. 16
3. 16
4. 15.9
5. 34
6. 55
7. 63
8. 53.2
9. 15.7 in.
10. 12.56 in.
11. 9.42 in.
12. 1
13. 1 1/3
14. 1 7/45
15. 1 1/5
16. 1 1/2
17. 7 1/2
18. 1 1/5
19. 1 1/27
20. 2 14/33

Page 95
1. 20
2. 18
3. 9
4. 23
5. 16
6. 63
7. 31
8. 22
9. 45
10. 23
11. 12
12. 25
13. 17.5 sq. units
14. 12 sq. units
15. 8 sq. units
16. 176.28
17. 2.19584
18. 345,870
19. 47,001.6
20. 4.7794
21. 28,944
22. 213.5328
23. 4.49686

Page 96
1. 8.5
2. 3.2
3. 35
4. 11.5
5. 10.2
6. 42
7. 34.1
8. 41.5
9. 27.5
10. 6.8
11. 3.4
12. 15
13. 1/4
14. 1/8
15. 3/8
16. 3/4
17. 3/5
18. 5/8
19. 1/5
20. 4/5
21. 7/8
22. 18/35
23. 53/90
24. 17/20
25. 1 5/18
26. 1 5/21
27. 1 19/45
28. 1 29/63
29. 5 1/2

Page 97
1. 9.2
2. 9.9
3. 44
4. 185
5. 85
6. 106
7. 90
8. 63
9. 25
10. 9
11. 43
12. 66.7
13. 51.4
14. 27.375
15. 5.3
16. 85
17. 87.1
18. 48.25
19. 16.67
20. 4
21. 6.67
22. 60
23. 8
24. 3.75
25. 20.25
26. 3.5
27. 31.5

Page 98
1. 19.5
2. 18
3. 77
4. 104.5
5. 21.2
6. 64.8
7. 57.9
8. 10.89
9. 13.1
10. 49.5
11. 23.9
12. 198
13. 78.5 sq. in.
14. 153.86 sq. in.
15. 28.26 sq. in.
16. 50.8
17. 194 r4
18. 14,518.519
19. 30 r6
20. 841,500
21. 2.4
22. 8 r65
23. 155.9
24. 13,093.3

Page 99
1. 3
2. 4.5
3. 5
4. 2.13
5. 3
6. 6
7. 8
8. 6
9. 2.5
10. 8.8
11. 9
12. 6
13. Shapes will vary.
14. Shapes will vary.
15. Shapes will vary.
16. 10.125
17. 6.67
18. 6
19. 14
20. 6
21. 8.75
22. 7.7
23. 4.4
24. 22.5

Page 100
1. 12
2. 7.2
3. 3.5
4. 5
5. 2.5
6. 3.5
7. 3
8. 3.5
9. 7.7
10. 7
11. 1.25
12. 7.5
13. $\overline{AH}$, CG, DE
14. DE
15. I
16. CI, BI, FI, GI
17. CG
18. FG
19. ∠FIG, ∠CIF, ∠CIB
20. IG
21. 9/14
22. 2 4/5
23. 14 14/15
24. 15/32
25. 2/7
26. 1
27. 1
28. 1 1/8
29. 5/9

Page 101
1. 42
2. 12
3. 20
4. 56
5. 15
6. 39
7. 37.5
8. 16
9. 18.75
10. 30
11. 45
12. 54
13. 9/10
14. 5/8
15. 4/5
16. 1/8
17. 3/5
18. 1/2
19. 1/4
20. 3/4
21. 233.1
22. 10,042
23. 8,234
24. 22.68
25. 92.03
26. 89

Page 102
1. 31.5
2. 44
3. 53.9
4. 12.6
5. 22
6. 22.5
7. 28
8. 18
9. 72
10. 65
11. 13
12. 42
13. 45°
14. 25°
15. 95°
16. 1
17. 4 2/3
18. 1 13/14
19. 4 1/6
20. 1 37/40
21. 1 11/15
22. 48/49
23. 1
24. 1 29/56

Page 103
1. 6
2. 60
3. 115
4. 10
5. 16
6. 14
7. 48
8. 41
9. 32
10. 4.25
11. 10
12. 32
13. 72 sq. in.
14. 45 sq. in.
15. 85.5 sq. in.
16. 22
17. 84
18. 86
19. 83.8

Page 104

1. 18
2. 32
3. 392
4. 82
5. 12
6. 110
7. 4.5
8. 82.8
9. 143
10. 44
11. 20
12. 26
13. Shapes will vary.
14. Shapes will vary.
15. Shapes will vary.
16. Shapes will vary.
17. 6
18. 4
19. 12.5
20. 21
21. 4.8
22. 12.5
23. 3
24. 12
25. 2

Page 105

1. -76
2. 14
3. 6
4. -25
5. 34
6. 37
7. -14
8. -78
9. 57
10. -29
11. 15
12. -5
13. 1/4
14. 3/4
15. 1/3
16. 1/2
17. 2/5
18. 3/5
19. 2/25
20. 3/25
21. 11/20
22. 10
23. 64
24. 103
25. 58
26. 6.8
27. 48
28. 71
29. 7
30. 9.5

Page 106

1. 0
2. 4
3. 1
4. 0
5. 1
6. 1
7. 0
8. 17
9. 0
10. -23
11. 0
12. 1
13. 63°
14. 36°
15. 27°
16. 9.099
17. 523.13
18. 1,478
19. 17.16
20. 4.93
21. 133
22. 5,465
23. 11,143

Page 107

1. -100
2. -56
3. -85
4. 22
5. -43
6. -26
7. -29
8. 76
9. 56
10. -59
11. 58
12. 1
13. 17.27 in.
14. 14.13 in.
15. 10.99 in.
16. 7/20
17. 4 2/3
18. 12 8/9
19. 1 7/8
20. 4/5
21. 15 1/6
22. 7/18
23. 9
24. 17 47/56

Bonus Box: 9 different outfits

Page 108

1. -103
2. -26
3. -35
4. -12
5. -25
6. 129
7. 13
8. -58
9. 21
10. 1
11. -1
12. -14
13. a, b
14. a, b, c, d, e, f
15. a, b, d, e
16. c, f
17. b
18. b, d
19. 11/20
20. 4/21
21. 5/126
22. 1 13/30
23. 5/12
24. 27/28
25. 62/63
26. 37/56
27. 4 7/8

Page 109

1. -44
2. -31
3. -65
4. 72
5. 24
6. -50
7. 21
8. -8
9. -18
10. -22
11. 171
12. -5
13. 128.74 mm
14. 116.18 mm
15. 87.92 mm
16. 24
17. 65
18. 65
19. 62.1

Page 110

1. -10
2. 12
3. 12
4. 16
5. 6
6. -20
7. 3
8. 5
9. 9
10. 9
11. 37
12. 10
13. 346.185 sq. mm
14. 615.44 sq. mm
15. 1,256 sq. mm
16. 11
17. 65
18. 108
19. 22
20. 2.3
21. 119
22. 46.875
23. 5.2
24. 16.5

Page 111

1. 12
2. -70
3. 28
4. -360
5. 180
6. 102
7. -51
8. 42
9. 0
10. -252
11. -325
12. 143
13. supplementary
14. supplementary
15. vertical
16. vertical
17. corresponding
18. corresponding
19. vertical
20. supplementary
21. 11.25
22. 3.5
23. 15
24. 16
25. 5
26. 80
27. 16
28. 126
29. 6